# Counting On Fingers

## Why Some Bright And Creative People Struggle With Numbers And Mathematics,

## And How That Can Be Changed

RICHARD WHITEHEAD

WITH

RONALD D. DAVIS

ISBN: 1912355078

ISBN-13: 978-1912355075

Cover design by Michaël Amos http://michaelamos.uk/

First edition, September 2023

Published by Create-A-Word Books Ltd
47 – 49 Church Street, Malvern, Worcestershire WR14 2AA,
United Kingdom

Visit www.whytyrannosaurusbutnotif.com

'The creative process and the learning process, if not the same thing, are so closely associated, we will never be able to separate them.'

— Ronald D. Davis.

# Table of Contents

# TABLE OF FIGURES

# ACKNOWLEDGMENTS

My heartfelt thanks go to all the dear friends and colleagues without whose help, advice and collaboration this book would not have come about.

Especial thanks to Axel Gudmundsson, Belinda Pollock, Larry Smith, Margot Young and Stacey Smith for their assistance in formatting the scripted exercises.

And to my two angels — Margarita in heaven, and Tatiana on earth — for all their loving patience, encouragement and support.

# A Note from Ron Davis

When I was an infant, my mother was told I was a 'Kanner's baby'. Dr. Leo Kanner coined the word autism in the US. For the first nine years of my life, I was oblivious to everything. I wasn't even aware that I was alive.

During part of my first eleven years, I had to go to school. I spent most of my time in the back of the classroom sitting in a corner, facing the wall. At the age of twelve I still hadn't learned a thing in school — not even the alphabet. My mother worked on me every day trying to teach me the Alphabet Song. She even tried to teach it to me in German. I couldn't learn the song past the first few letters.

Mathematics, however, was different. Not because I was taught it well. Numbers and I have always been good friends, so I assimilated mathematics without being taught it.

I cannot remember a time when a quadratic equation did not evoke within me a feeling of comfort. Maybe it is the shape of a square, or the idea of a limit to higher powers of unknown quantities, or maybe it's just because I think with pictures and it's easy to think with shapes and quantities. If you can think with shapes and quantities, you could invent your own mathematics.

At the age of 38, a personal breakthrough led me from being functionally illiterate to reading a book — *Treasure Island*, by Robert Louis Stevenson — from cover to cover in a single sitting. It was the first time in my life that I had read an entire book. Over a short period of time, this personal discovery led to a complete set of methods to enable dyslexic individuals to read with ease and accuracy.

As I set about helping dyslexics to become readers, I discovered that there are also smart, picture-thinking individuals who struggle with numbers. Some of them are dyslexic as well; some of them 'just' dyscalculic. Despite never being numerically challenged myself, my dyslexic and autistic background enabled me to identify the missing pieces in a person's development and learning that can lead to number blindness.

Over the past thirty years, hundreds of remarkable individuals have joined me in my quest to unlock learning for the little boy or girl in the corner who thinks and learns differently, and who the people teaching them often do not know how to help. I commend this book to you as a comprehensive account of what we have found out about people who struggle with numbers, why they do so, and how that can be changed.

# Preface

Here is a book about number sense written by... a linguist. When at school, I was very good at languages and went on to study two of them at university. I was also 'okay' at mathematics. But whereas I could write an error-free essay in German on animal rights, mass unemployment, or why you should visit the Black Forest, every maths assignment I handed in had some 'careless' mistakes. At the age of 15, I had a good friend in my maths class whose work was always handed back with a big '99%' written on it; mine typically came back with '85%' and fifteen reasons to face-palm. So when the time came to choose my Sixth Form specialisms, Goethe, the Rhineland and separable verbs won hands-down over statistics, trigonometry and calculus.

This begs the question: why am I writing a book about maths difficulties? An elaborate exercise in impostor syndrome? Perhaps. Yet despite never becoming a 'proper' mathematician, I always found mathematics fascinating. I remember vividly how, when I was off school with a protracted illness at the age of nine, I got hold of a note book, wrote out all the square numbers up to 144 *for fun* (in those long-gone days of three TV channels and no Internet, we had an adaptive approach to finding entertainment, didn't we...?), and suddenly realised that the difference between each consecutive pair of square numbers increased by two. 4 – 1 is 3; 9 – 4 is 5; 16 – 9 is 7, and so on. (It was only years later, with the help of the Davis methods and its clay-based approach to mathematics, that I worked out why...). Once convalesced, I returned triumphantly to school knowing this fact, all the powers of 2 up to 8192, and several other numerical gems. I cannot remember if I boasted. Certainly, my new-found knowledge did not make me any new friends.

Later, in my early thirties, I became interested in dyslexia and fascinated with the Davis Dyslexia methods, a ground-breaking approach that sees dyslexia as rooted in perceptual talent rather than a disability. In the course of my training, I was introduced to the Davis approach to dyscalculia — dyslexia's mathematical cousin — and was hooked. I loved the simple elegance of laying out one hundred clay balls in a 10 x 10 grid to master the times tables by 'seeing' them. As I worked with more and more individuals on their maths difficulties, and saw rapid and remarkable progress, I started to specialise in how individuals with dyscalculia naturally think, and therefore learn.

My own teenage glitchiness in maths assignments gave me some clues too. Rather than working with robotic consistency, the human mind switches constantly between different modes of operation. The more often your mind flits creatively between different thoughts, the more likely you are to forget where you put your keys, leave your toothbrush at home when going on holiday, or make a mistake in a linear maths task. In my life to date, I have done all three a good few times.

In his own childhood, Ron Davis was much better than me at mathematics, but much worse at reading and writing. Initially, also, at speaking and remembering. Profoundly autistic until the age of 9, functionally illiterate until the age of 38, but mathematically savant and with a genius IQ, Davis developed a remarkable understanding of his own dyslexic and autistic thinking processes. Approaching learning difficulties uniquely from the inside out, Davis brings us crucial new insights into the different states of our mind and how to marshal our mental faculties to succeed in the task in hand. Davis's own learning journey, emerging from mute autistic childhood, through dyslexic adolescence and adulthood, to become a fluent reader and author of multiple books, has enabled him to identify the missing pieces that make learning difficult. And how to help a person fill them in, so that learning becomes easy.

— Richard Whitehead

# Chapter 1: The Importance of Numeracy

In 2017, a few weeks before a general election, a prominent UK politician made a mistake. The mistake was made in a live interview; it was mathematical rather than political and, as such, much harder to hide.

Shadow Home Secretary Diane Abbott announced that her party, if elected, would recruit 10,000 new police officers at a cost of £300,000 — the equivalent of a £30 annual salary per police officer.

The interviewer immediately queried the figures: '£300,000 for 10,000 police officers? What are you paying them?'

Abbott laughed embarrassedly and corrected her costings to £80 million. This, too, was questioned by the interviewer, who pointed out that this would still amount to a miserly £8000 annual salary per officer recruited.

Abbott then went on to explain that the officers would be recruited over a four-year period, 'recruiting 25,000 extra police officers a year at least'. Later in the interview, the numbers changed again: 'The figures are that the additional costs in Year One when we anticipate recruiting about 250,000 policemen will be £64.3 million.'

Of course, Abbott was not planning to turn the UK into a penurious police state. Her party was not about to recruit one million UK citizens to serve as police officers on a salary of £257.20 per year each. Subsequently, Abbott explained that she was suffering from Type 2 diabetes and that this, combined with the pressures of a gruelling election campaign, had affected aspects of her lucidity. Assuming this was indeed the case, her treatment at the hands of some of the media after the mishap was nothing short of cruel. Just like the rest of us, politicians are allowed to be human, to mis-speak, to have a bad day and to fall ill.

Nonetheless, the Abbott incident provides a stark illustration of an important point. If a Cambridge University History graduate and eloquent politician of many decades' experience can cite figures in a public broadcast for which a maths teacher would give *nul points* to a twelve-year-old, it all goes to show that intelligence is not a single 'thing' that can be measured on a linear IQ scale. Like the sliding controls on a sophisticated audio recording device, our intelligence is a complex interplay between a number of ways in which we take in, categorise, analyse, deduce, and innovate. And what is more, each aspect of our intelligence can have a 'good day' or a 'bad day', depending on how robustly it is built to withstand issues that impact on our day-to-day well-being.

The idea of multiple intelligences is not new. First proposed by Howard Gardner in 1983 [1] , multiple intelligence theory maintains that intelligence cannot be measured on a single linear scale but, rather, consists of many distinct components, each of which can be developed to its own particular level within the same individual. Though disputed by some, multiple intelligence theory makes sense to anyone who knows, for instance, a linguist (such as me) who cannot kick a ball or put up shelves, a mathematician who writes awful poems, a numerically challenged artist, a tone-deaf engineer, or a software developer who stands in the corner alone at cocktail parties. Multiple intelligence theory has played an important role in exploding the cruel myth that there are 'clever' people and 'stupid' people. It has made us much more intelligent about intelligence.

However, multiple intelligence theory on its own is not much use to a parent or an educator. Telling a maths teacher that their most failing student may actually be very good at dance, embroidery or horse-riding will be neither revelatory nor cathartic. When multiple intelligence theory is reduced to an 'everyone-is-good-at-something' statement in scientific packaging, it is just another form of learning disability theory with a comfort blanket attached. 'There, there — it's a shame that you can't count — but don't worry, neither could Henry Winkler — and it didn't stop him becoming an actor.'

---

[1] (Gardner, 2011)

This book will try to be more interesting than that. Rather than treating mathematical difficulties as a life sentence, it will demonstrate that even the most severe forms of dyscalculia can be addressed using the individual's *existing cognitive and intellectual assets*. Rather than telling bright but struggling mathematicians to 'buy a pocket calculator and go and find something you're good at', it is supremely important to consider how mathematical learning can be repackaged to play to these individuals' natural and often considerable strengths.

Why supremely important? Because a pocket calculator does not replace mathematical intuition. In the supermarket, in the clothes shop, ordering pizzas for an office party, timing a journey, working out what monthly data package to get for our phone, deciding whether to pay upfront or in monthly instalments for our car insurance, we find ourselves taking snap decisions based on more or less sensible estimations. If we are starting or running a business, these scenarios can be multiplied many times over, in both frequency and import. Poor numeracy, if not addressed, can be a lifelong curse. While business insolvency, personal bankruptcy, rent arrears, unpunctuality, spoilt meals and missed deadlines can have a variety of causes, problems with counting, measuring, timing and mathematical logic will certainly not help. Like it or not, that is why the media pressed Abbott so relentlessly on her misspoken figures. When politicians get elected to power, they take control of billions of pounds of our taxes. The idea that they may not be able to count freaks us, frankly, out.

In February 2022, 12-year-old Rory and his mother were very worried. Rory had just received the results of his Mathematics Common Entrance Trial Examination: 22%. To receive a place at the senior school that he dearly wanted to attend, he would need to more than double his marks in the space of three months.

In March, Rory was assessed by an educational psychologist. His Number Operations were found to be at 2nd percentile. For readers unfamiliar with percentiles, a 2nd percentile score indicates that 98% of people of your age perform better than you do.

In April, Rory came to me for a 48-hour intensive Davis Maths Mastery Programme. This quietly revolutionary intervention enables bright, creative, but numerically challenged individuals to become mathematically confident and competent, step-by-step, in specially tailored ways that play to their natural strengths. As Rory worked through the programme, he became rapidly numerate. He found not just that he was able to perform mental and written arithmetic much more accurately and fluently, but that the revision coaching he was receiving from his maths teacher was now making much more sense to him.

In May 2022, Rory took the Common Entrance Examination and passed Mathematics with 65%. He was accepted by the school that he wanted to attend.

Rory's story is markedly similar to Clara's. In 2006, aged 30, Clara wanted to study nursing at a local college of further education. Because of the importance of accurately measuring doses, comparing treatment risks, interpreting screen test results, and so on, healthcare workers need to be numerate. When I met Clara, she was devastated for two reasons. Firstly, she had failed the Access to Nursing Mathematics test, obtaining 19%. Secondly, by way of investigating the failure, her college had arranged an educational psychologist assessment to ascertain whether she might be dyslexic. As none of her assessment scores had been particularly high, the assessor had concluded that dyslexia was not indicated, just limited overall intelligence. I recall Clara repeating to me again and again, 'She basically said I'm not dyslexic, I'm just stupid.'

Except she wasn't. Six weeks and a Davis Maths Mastery Programme later, Clara retook the Access to Nursing Mathematics Test and passed with over 60%. When her college tutor contacted the assessor to enquire how a person of limited intelligence could improve her mathematical ability by more than 40% in six weeks, the assessor revised the report and allowed Clara to be dyslexic after all.

Whether we call it dyscalculia, 'maths dyslexia' or 'not good with figures', a mathematics and numeracy deficit is not a life sentence. Rather, it is the product of mis-steps in the nature, speed and/or sequencing of a person's mathematical learning in the early years of their schooling. Before a child can successfully be taught maths, they need to be *thinking mathematically*. Children develop mathematical thinking at differing speeds from one another, and some need outside assistance in developing it. If you try to teach symbol-based mathematical *operations* to a child who hasn't yet developed mathematical *thinking*, you will get rote-learnt answers at best, and confusion and 'hit-and-miss' answers at worst. In all cases, there will be an impact on self-esteem and a conclusion that 'maths is not for me'. A conclusion, in my experience, that is entirely and tragically wrong.

# Chapter 2: What Stops Numeracy? An Exploration of Dyscalculia

Dyscalculia is dyslexia's poor cousin. While dyslexia is widely known, talked about, and increasingly celebrated for the talents that accompany it, comparatively few of us have heard of dyscalculia.

What is more, under current UK guidance, problems with mathematics do not automatically make you dyscalculic. SASC is the UK's SpLD Assessment Standards Committee. The initials within the initials (SpLD) stand for Specific Learning Difficulties. SASC identifies three categories of mathematics learning difficulties:

1. Dyscalculia – a SpLD whose core feature is a problem with sense of number
2. Other SpLDs which do not include a problem with sense of number, but which may have an impact upon mathematics learning
3. Maths learning difficulties arising from lack of appropriate teaching, environmental factors or other medical conditions.[2]

---

[2] (SpLD Assessments Standards Committee (SASC), 2019)

Whatever system of nomenclature one might choose to use, the prevalence of numeracy difficulties among the UK population would appear to be substantial. In 2011, the Department for Business, Innovation and Skills found that 49.1% of UK adults aged 16 – 65 have numeracy skills at Entry level 3 or below.[3] Broadly speaking, Entry Level 3 is the level of literacy and/or numeracy that would be expected from a typical 9 – 11 year old child. In an online survey of 2007 adults aged 16 to 75, conducted in 2019 in the UK by the polling agency Ipsos MORI, in partnership with the Policy Institute at King's College London and National Numeracy, one in four respondents said they would be deterred from applying for a job if it listed using numbers and data as a requirement. In the same survey, 31% of respondents stated that they are 'not a numbers person'. Significantly more women (38%) than men (23%) stated this. What is more, 29% of female respondents stated that mathematics and numbers made them anxious, as compared with 13% of male respondents.[4]

These figures would suggest that the number of adults with numeracy difficulties might actually be greater than the number of those who struggle with literacy - even though the latter are much more talked about than the former.

In the case of learners with numeracy difficulties, educators have two options. One is to write off the learner as permanently numerically challenged and to teach

---

[3] (Department for Business, Innovation and Skills, 2012)
[4] (National Numeracy, 2019)

coping strategies based around devices such as rote-learning and mnemonics. I have seen this approach taken all too often by well-meaning teachers who, feeling unequipped to assist a child to become numerate, decided that the best they could do for them was to get them through the next test, end-of-year exam, public exam or other formal milestone. We might call this the 'sick-on-the-floor' approach if we name it after the common aide-memoire taught for 8 x 8 = 64: 'I ate and ate and was sick on the floor'.

The other option is to analyse the nature of a person's numeracy difficulties, with a belief that they can be remedied. Doing this requires us to assess the nature of numeracy difficulties alongside any typical *strengths* that a numerically challenged person may have. Only then can we figure out what the missing pieces are, why they are missing, and how to supply them in a way that plays to the person's natural strengths, thereby enabling them to 'stick'.

## Numeracy difficulties and working memory – a typical learner profile

The first step in designing a solution for numerically challenged individuals must be to gain an understanding of how such individuals typically think and, therefore, learn. This will be done here in two ways. First, we will take a technical look at the question from an academic standpoint, reviewing some of the key research into the learning profiles of people who struggle with mathematics.

After that, we will take a more subjective look based on personal observations made while helping people with numeracy difficulties to overcome them.

## The 'techie' view: general intelligence, working memory, and rapid automatised naming

A learner with numeracy difficulties is not a learner of low intelligence. In a study of 140 eleven-year-old children with developmental dyscalculia, Gross-Tsur, Manor and Shalev (1996) found that IQ scores ranged from 80 to 129, with a mean of 98.2. [5] For readers not familiar with standardised IQ scoring, this means that these children's IQs ranged from 9th percentile (i.e. 91 out of 100 children of the same age would have higher IQs) to 97th percentile (meaning only 3 out of 100 children would have higher IQs), and the mean was around 46th percentile, which is firmly average (50th percentile would be bang on the general population mean). In 2010, Tracy and Ross Alloway found that IQ in children at five years of age was not a reliable predictor of either literacy or numeracy skills six years later.[6]

In actual fact, the best predictor of numeracy skills would appear to be working memory. Working memory is a construct devised by British psychologists Alan Baddeley and Graham Hitch in the 1970s. It is essentially a measure of how much information a person can hold in their short-

---

[5] (Gross-Tsur, et al., 1996)
[6] (Alloway & Alloway, 2010)

term memory and manipulate mentally. Solving riddles, remembering what to buy in the grocery store, remembering the directions you got from a passer-by until you have successfully reached your destination are all underpinned by working memory. And so, for that matter, is mental arithmetic.

In 1986, Baddeley proposed that working memory consists of four components. The phonological loop is our mind's ability to function like an MP3 record and playback device, holding snippets of verbal information in a kind of short-term mental soundtrack which is deleted once the information is no longer needed. The visuospatial sketchpad is our mind's ability to hold information about what-is-where — remembering where we parked our car so we can find it again once we're done shopping, for instance. The central executive is a supervisory system that orchestrates the previous two; and the episodic buffer is a kind of record-keeper or story-teller that draws information from our various senses along with the phonological loop and visuospatial sketchpad, as well as from our long-term memory, binding together the various strands into an episode which, depending on its significance to the individual, may be stored in long-term memory.[7]

In 2003, a group of researchers led by Minna Kyttälä at the University of Turku in Finland established a strong link between visuospatial working memory and counting skills

---

[7] (Baddeley, 1986)

in pre-schoolers. [8] Five years later, Kyttälä found a similarly strong correlation between visuospatial working memory and numeracy skills in 15 – 16 year olds. [9] Researchers Klein and Bisanz [10] and Witt [11] found correlations between visuo-spatial sketchpad capacity on the one hand, and addition and subtraction on the other. Witt additionally found correlations between the phonological loop and multiplication tasks. In a study conducted in Italy (specifically Cagliari, Sardinia), Fanari, Meloni and Massidda (2019) found that spatial working memory at the beginning of first grade influenced early numerical skills, which in turn influenced mathematical performance at the end of first grade. At the end of second grade, they found a direct correlation between visual and spatial working memory on the one hand and mathematical ability on the other. [12]

The idea that a strong working memory would be an asset in mathematical tasks is common sense. If working memory is defined as 'the system or mechanism underlying the maintenance of task-relevant information during the performance of a cognitive task' [13], then any form of mental arithmetic must be reliant upon it, as must any mental processes undertaken while addressing a word-based mathematical task, as well as the mental

---

[8] (Kyttälä, et al., 2003)

[9] (Kyttälä, 2008)

[10] (Klein & Bisanz, 2000)

[11] (Witt, 2006)

[12] (Fanari, et al., 2019)

[13] (Miyake & Shah, 1999)

organisation required to address multi-step mathematical procedures such as complex algebraic equations.

Even when mathematical tasks are performed on paper, each individual component of the process is still reliant on either mental arithmetic or rote-learnt material. For example, a triple-digit multiplication sum might be solved on paper, but the paper is simply the place where you write each of the three single-digit multiplications that the process comprises. And each of these must either be solved mentally or must be recalled from learnt times tables.

Another cognitive function that has been investigated for a link to mathematical difficulties is Rapid Automatised Naming (RAN). RAN is our ability to 'reel off' simple pieces of data that we learnt when we were young — such as letters, digits, or the names of colours. A number of studies have looked at, and proposed, a link between RAN and dyslexia. In 2012, Elizabeth Norton and Maryanne Wolf suggested that RAN measures act as a microcosm of the reading system and act as a robust early predictor of reading ability — in other words, that young pre-reader children who struggle to name letters and numbers at speed are almost certainly going to struggle with reading when they get older.[14]

However, dyscalculia would seem to differ from dyslexia here. In 2018, a group of Chilean and Spanish researchers, headed by Bárbara Guzmán, investigated the

---

[14] (Norton & Wolf, 2012)

contribution of working memory and Rapid Automatized Naming (RAN) to growth trajectories in number processing.[15] The participants in their study were two groups of 32 first-grade children in Chile: one group were at risk of developing mathematical learning disabilities (called 'MLD' in this study), while the other group comprised typically developing children ('non-MLD'). The researchers tested the subjects' ability to name lists of digits forwards and in reverse order. They also tested the subjects' speed of naming a list of letters (RAN-letter) and a list of digits (RAN-digit). The children's numerical ability was tested on three occasions: in May, September and December of the first grade. (December is the end of the school year in Chile). The working memory and RAN testing was conducted on the last of the three visits.

Guzmán's team found no correlation between rapid digit naming or forward digit naming and the development of numerical ability. When it came to backward digit naming, however, they did find a direct correlation: the children who struggled with this task were the children with the greatest numeracy difficulties. The researchers point out that, whereas forward digit naming typically involves a person's phonological loop (see above), backward digit naming involves the central executive: you can't just 'play back' the 'echo' of the digits that you just heard; rather, you have to gather them in your working memory, reverse them, and then say them.

---

[15] (Guzmán, et al., 2019)

However, it was the results for RAN testing that were particularly intriguing. The researchers found no connection between the subjects' RAN-digit ability and the development of their numeracy. They did find a connection between RAN-letter and numeracy development, but only among the typical learners; not among the MLD-group. In other words, non-MLD children who did not have a mathematical learning disability performed especially well at mathematics if they were speedy at naming letters; but for those in the MLD group, letter-naming speed had no bearing on numerical ability.

Drawing together the research by Norton/Wolf and by Guzmán's team, we can conclude: if a child is slow at naming digits and letters, they are likely to develop dyslexia. But dyscalculics include both slow namers and speedy namers.

Earlier, in 2008, research led by Edith Willburger highlighted the same difference between dyslexia and dyscalculia when it comes to RAN.[16] Willburger's team conducted separate testing on dyslexic-but-not-dyscalculic, dyscalculic-but-not dyslexic, and dyslexic-and-dyscalculic schoolchildren, as well as on controls with no recorded learning challenges. All the test subjects were in Grades 2 — 4 of various primary schools in Salzburg, Austria. The total pool of children screened was 1046, with roughly equal numbers of boys and girls. They established that, while all the dyslexic subjects (with or without

---

[16] (Willburger, et al., 2008)

dyscalculia) exhibited general RAN difficulties, the dyscalculic-but-not-dyslexic subjects had a RAN deficit in the naming of quantities, but not in the naming of other categories of items.

It is particularly interesting that, just like in the Chilean study cited above, these children had no deficit, compared to the controls, in the naming of digits. Naming digits is quite different from naming quantities. The former requires you just to know what a digit symbol is called; the latter requires either counting or a mysterious process known as 'subitising', which is the human ability to recognise a quantity of five or less items without actually counting the individual items.

All of this gives us some important clues as to what we might call the nature of knowing in mathematics. The story so far: the strength of a person's working memory, especially their central executive, appears to correlate closely to their numeracy. However, there is no correlation between dyscalculia and a person's speed of naming stimuli (unless counting of the stimuli is required). Whereas Rapid Automatised Naming is a simple regurgitation of learnt material, working memory is about actively manipulating information in your mind. Simply put: numerically challenged individuals do not need to be taught to be better at rote-learning or parroting — they are already as good at this as the next person. Rather, their challenges are linked to glitches that are occurring when they work creatively with quantities in their minds.

Now let us follow these clues a little further. Let us invent a child, whom we will call Manfred. Our imaginary Manfred was in Willburger's screening group. He struggles with arithmetic but not with reading and writing. Like most dyscalculic individuals (see above), his working memory has limitations. By contrast, his Rapid Automatised Naming tested as in the normal range for everything except quantities. He can reel off digits and letters at a decent rate.

Yet Manfred is struggling to learn the times tables. (If he wasn't, he would be unlikely to be included in the dyscalculic group of the study.) Over and over again, his teachers have tried to teach him, and he has tried to learn them. Why can he rapidly-automatisedly-name letters and digits, but not multiplication facts?

Well, Manfred is slow to name quantities. And the *meaning* of the times tables is rooted in quantities; multiplying is about replicating a given quantity a certain number of times. If Manfred were able to learn the times tables as a series of numeral names and words without focusing on their meaning — a bit like learning and reciting Lewis Carroll's nonsense poem 'Jabberwocky' — his RAN fluency in naming familiar things like digits and letters might be enough.

But it isn't. Manfred cannot learn twelve sets of times tables as if they were twelve nonsense poems. Here's the deal: effective long-term memorisation of mathematical data can only take place when the answers *make sense*.

In 2012, a team of researchers led by Terezinha Nunes published the results of an investigation into how mathematical reasoning and (memorised) arithmetic abilities contribute to mathematical achievement at UK Key Stages 2 and 3.[17] They worked with 2,579 Key Stage 2 and 1,680 Key Stage 3 children whose achievement at school to date had been tracked as part of an existing longitudinal study. (Longitudinal studies are research projects that track the development of children or adults over a number of years.) Nunes and her team tested each of these children using an existing standardised test of arithmetic and a test of mathematical reasoning that Nunes herself had devised. They then cross-referenced the results with the pupils' existing school mathematics test results, taking into account factors of age, working memory and general IQ.

The team found that mathematical reasoning and (memorised) arithmetic both made independent contributions to the prediction of achievement in Key Stage 2 and 3 mathematics, but that mathematical reasoning was by far the stronger predictor of the two. In other words, to do well at mathematics in school, at least up to the age of fourteen, it is more important to be able to think mathematically than to be able to rote-learn times tables and other mathematical facts.

A number of years ago, I worked extensively one-to-one with a fifteen-year-old girl, whom we shall call Geraldine,

---

[17] (Nunes, et al., 2012)

on her numeracy and mathematical ability. She had tested as having average processing speed but below-average working memory. During several sessions, we worked on building up her mastery of the times tables with a grid made from 100 balls of plasticine, laid out as a 10x10 square. This grid is used in the Davis Maths Mastery Programme, about which more will follow later in this book. In these sessions, various rectangular sections of the grid would be cordoned off using plasticine 'ropes' so that the answer to a multiplication sum could be seen and explored. Here is an example:

$$8 \times 3 = 24$$

*Fig. 1: The Davis Multiplication Grid*

In the early stages of our work, I was struck by the negative interference of Geraldine's attempts to recall the times tables from memory. Even with the ball grid in front of her, she initially tended to ignore it, look up into the air, and try to recall the answer from memory. Almost invariably, she would do so incorrectly. It took multiple, playfully bossy interventions from me — 'Uh-uh, look down here (pointing at the ball grid) — the answer's here!' — before she started to relax into simply observing the balls and counting to obtain an answer. Then, in the later sessions, I guided her towards using logic to work out the answers creatively — for example, when finding the answer to 6 x 6, she would lay down an extra rope to separate 5 x 6 balls from 1 x 6 balls. She was familiar with the 5 times table, so could easily see that she was adding 6 balls to 30 balls to obtain 36:

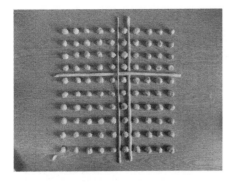

*Fig. 2: seeing 6 x 6 as 5 x 6 + 1 x 6*

In doing so, Geraldine was developing her mathematical reasoning as well as applying personal creativity to solving multiplication problems. After that, rather quickly, she became ever more confident and correct in her answers to times table questions.

### *The human view: the dyscalculic thinking style*

Examining statistics about the mental strengths and challenges of dyscalculic individuals is one thing. Knowing dyscalculics personally — a lot of them — is another. Alongside many of my fellow Davis Dyslexia Programme Facilitators, I have worked with scores of individuals — intensively, one-to-one — to help them to overcome their difficulties with numeracy and mathematics.

Of course, every numerically challenged individual who comes our way has their own unique profile, personality, and life experiences. Nonetheless, these individuals tend to exhibit a common set of mental traits and characteristics that we might refer to as the *dyscalculic thinking style*.

#### Picture Thinking

In his book, 'The Gift of Dyslexia,' Ronald Davis identifies two fundamentally different styles of thinking: word thinking and picture thinking.[18] Word thinking is sometimes also referred to as internal monologue; it is the ability to think with the sounds of words in your mind. By contrast, picture thinking is the ability to think directly with visual, tactile and/or other sensory 'images'. When you are travelling to your great-aunt's 90th birthday party and mentally rehearsing your words of congratulation to

---

[18] (Davis & Braun, 2010)

her, you are doing word thinking. When you picture the best way to drive from your home to a friends' house, imagine what it feels like to stroke your cat, or imagine what the soup you are cooking would taste like with a little more salt and garlic, you are doing picture thinking.

Word thinking is naturally linear: if you are talking to yourself in your head, your 'thought sentences' will exist in time as a linear process with a beginning, middle and end. A mental image, by contrast, exists in space; each individual element will have its own place within the image, and multiple elements can coexist at the same time. As such, mental imagery is much more associative than linear.

While working in learning support in a secondary school, I vividly remember working with a then 18-year-old boy with a diagnosis of ADHD. He was known by teachers and fellow-pupils alike as a 'rambler': in a single conversation, he would roam widely across a vast array of different topics, and he would quickly lose track of the original matter under discussion. The boy himself was aware of this. 'My mind works like a mind map,' he once said to me. 'One thought can spark multiple new thoughts at the same time, then I pick one of them and it creates a load of new thoughts, then I pick one of them, and so on. And that can very quickly take me far away from the first thought, so I forget what it was.'

Dyslexics, too, excel at picture thinking. At some point in their life, they sometimes acquire a modicum of word thinking, but if they do so, it tends to be later in childhood than their non-dyslexic peers and it always plays second fiddle to picture thinking, which remains their primary imaginative and problem-solving tool. Some dyslexics never develop word thinking at all; I know this from the astonished reaction, 'What? There are people who do that??' from some adult dyslexic participants when introducing the concept at workshops or on parent courses. When learning to read, dyslexics invariably weren't 'doing' word thinking yet. This is the primary reason why phonic reading teaching did not work for them; that is a separate topic dealt with in some depth in my book, 'Why *Tyrannosaurus* But Not *If?*'[19]

In my experience, many individuals who struggle with mathematics are picture thinkers too. Typically, they present as creative, imaginative, sometimes impulsive individuals who are easily fired up by an idea or drift off into reveries. Famous people who struggled with maths are said to include creatives and innovators such as: the writer Hans Christian Andersen; the inventor Thomas Edison; singers Cher, Mick Hucknall and Robbie Williams; inventor and US founding father Benjamin Franklin; and actor and storywriter Henry Winkler.[20] The dyslexia and dyscalculia learning software providers IDL identify a 'dyscalculia superpower' consisting of creativity, strategic thinking, practical ability, problem solving, love of words and intuitive thinking.[21]

---

[19] (Whitehead, 2017)

[20] (Singh, 2021)

[21] (International Dyslexia Learning Solutions Limited, 2021)

A word of caution is needed here: picture thinking can also help you be very good at maths. Take Albert Einstein, who despite rumours to the contrary was an outstanding mathematician. Einstein notably said, 'The words of language, as they are written or spoken, do not seem to play any role in my mechanism of thought. The physical entities which seem to serve as elements in thought are certain signs and more or less clear images.'[22]

Mathematics is about the manipulation of quantities. Being able to 'see' quantities in your imagination, and how they change, could help a person succeed in mathematics. On the other hand, the associative, lateral nature of picture thinking could scramble the linear processes often required to solve a mathematical problem successfully.

### Disorientation

Davis also identifies another key to understanding why bright, creative individuals can struggle with aspects of academic learning. This can occur when such individuals become unusually adept at a mental function that Davis calls *disorientation*. In Davis theory, *orientation* is a state in which a person's mind sees what their eyes are seeing; it hears what their ears are hearing; their sense of balance is optimal and their sense of time is consistent. By contrast, disorientation is a state in which the mind creates

---

[22] (Einstein, 1995)

something internally and sees, hears or feels that as if it were reality.

A common instance of disorientation occurs to many of us when sitting in a stationary vehicle and looking at an adjacent vehicle that starts to move. When this occurs, you may well feel as if it is you who are moving. If the vehicle is a car and you are the driver, the feeling of movement can be so real that it can cause you to pump the footbrake. (This has happened to me.)

When this occurs, what you are experiencing is a rapid-response problem solving mechanism. When the adjacent vehicle moves off, your visual sense notices that your environment is shifting and informs your brain that you are moving. At the same time, your bodily sense continues to inform your brain that you are stationary. Your brain cannot compute how to respond to the impossible contradiction of being stationary and in motion at the same time; therefore, to avoid paralysis (or possibly something worse), it rapidly brings the senses back into harmony. It is better to make a mistake than to endure the paralysing contradiction. Generating and experiencing an albeit non-existent sense of movement at least gives the brain an exit door from the sensory conflict; once this is done, the brain can start reacting to the environment again and learning from it. If you disorientate into a false sense of movement, it usually does not last very long, as fresh data will soon emerge that will demonstrate that you are stationary.

Davis identifies a heightened disorientation ability as a key feature of dyslexia. Disorientation is activated by an individual, usually in infancy and as a problem-solving mechanism that helps a small child exit paralysing states of confusion and/or sensory conflict. When applied to the real, three-dimensional world, the mechanism brings more benefits than problems to the individual, hence it becomes automated as a quick-fire response to confusion stimuli. Once a child starts learning to read and write at school, the disorientation response is already automated and kicks in involuntarily whenever what is being taught is sufficiently confusing; however, when applied to two-dimensional textual symbols, disorientation just makes the confusion even worse.

A key symptom of disorientation is inconsistency of response. A dyslexic child prone to disorientation may read a word correctly on one line of a book, then read it incorrectly when it reoccurs a few lines later. The mind is flitting between orientation and disorientation — between accurate perception and creative manipulation of the environment — hence to the outside world, the individual's responses may look as if there is a 'loose connection' in the mind's processing system.

Whenever I work with individuals on their mathematical challenges, I see disorientation writ large. Even after many hours of one-to-one support, and after significant progress in mathematical ability has been achieved, my clients will still make sudden unpredictable errors on simple mathematical operations, amidst correct responses given to more complex ones.

Some clients also disappear into their own thoughts. During my first meeting with one boy, who subsequently made rapid progress in his arithmetical ability, he would frequently pause for a long time after I had asked a question, then respond with a 'Sorry — what?' What is generally known as absent-mindedness is actually a form of disorientation — the person's mind loses contact with what their eyes are seeing and ears are hearing and disappears into an alternate world, sometimes for a brief moment, other times for longer. As Psychology Today puts it, '... someone with dyscalculia may appear absent-minded, with a tendency to get lost, lose things, lose track of time, or easily become disoriented; because of this, it is possible for them to be diagnosed with ADHD rather than dyscalculia.'[23]

Successful mathematical problem-solving requires focusing stamina. The mathematician needs to be able to keep track of each element of the problem from the start through to the finish. A person who loses track of their car keys in the physical world might well lose track of the little numeral 1 that they carried in a column addition. While disorientation is a creative, problem-solving talent, the 'glitchiness' that it can bring to linear thought processes can be a big contributing factor in the development of mathematical difficulties.

---

[23] (Psychology Today, 2021)

*Challenges in Time and Space*

Dyscalculic difficulties invariably go hand-in-hand with difficulty telling the time. A child with mathematical challenges will almost always have struggled to learn to read a clock face at the appropriate age for doing so. They may be able to read the time on a digital display, but if the display is in the 24-hour clock, they will often struggle to convert it back to the 12-hour clock.

Learning to read digits on a clock display is not the same as 'knowing' time. Most dyscalculic individuals struggle to conceptualise time; they will not be able to estimate how long a task will take, and they will often struggle with punctuality and with deadlines.

Some dyscalculic individuals also struggle with personal organisation. Their personal spaces can be disorderly, and they can struggle with the steps required to de-clutter it.

These tendencies actually link back to the disorientation function mentioned earlier. As children grow up, they typically learn certain lessons from their physical environment. Occurrences in the physical world are rooted in *consequence* or causality — the relationship between *cause* and *effect*. Simply put: things make other things happen, and something that happens was caused to happen by something else.

When we perceive chains of consequence (something causes something else, then the something-else causes

29

something-else-else, and so on), we are actually perceiving a rudimentary form of *sequence*: things following each other, one after another.

Sequences of consequences occur across *time*. Different sequences of consequences take different amounts of time to complete: some take longer, others take less long. When we start to compare them, we are using time as an instrument to measure duration.

Everything in the physical world has a geolocation: a place where it exists in relation to everything else in 3D space. The place where something exists will determine the function it can fulfil. A car key in your pocket is useful; a car key dropped into a canal, less so. When you put a bunch of things in useful places, you experience creating *order*. Order is the way in which groups of things come together to perform a function. Of course, it isn't enough to put things in their proper places. They also need to be in their proper positions in those places — try pouring milk into an upside-down glass and you will see what I mean. What is more, the things need to be in their proper conditions — if the milk has gone off, you are unlikely to derive much pleasure from the resulting drink.

As mentioned above, these concepts permeate our existence in the physical world, hence most children assimilate them naturally as they grow older. However, some children spend protracted periods of time attuned, not to the physical world, but to their imagination. The more vivid a child's imagination is, the more often it will exceed what the physical world has to offer in excitement and stimulation. When attuned to our imagination, we are inhabiting a thought world that is not governed by cause, effect, time, sequence and order. In the words of Ronald Davis:

'For a child who habitually spends much time in an imaginary world, nothing permanently exists. His friends and enemies exist only for him. The scenarios that are acted out are real only to him. To others, he is just playing by himself. To him it is his reality — his life. Even though he is just playing, the life lessons learned are incorporated into his filtering system. In his imaginary world consequence doesn't exist; things just happen — and almost anything can — at his whim and direction.'[24]

---

[24] (Davis & Braun, 2003)

# Chapter 3: Thinking Mathematically

For a child with incomplete mastery of the physical world concepts of cause, effect, time, sequence and order, the mathematical 'world' is not going to make much sense either. Take this simple equation:

$$2 + 1 = 3$$

In essence, a mathematical equation is an expression of *change*. At the beginning, there are two; at the end, there are three. Here, the type of change occurring is *adding*. To add two quantities is to bring them together in the same place, so they become a single quantity. The reason *why* we have three is because one was added to two. Therefore, a mathematical equation is also an expression of *consequence*: one can identify a *cause* (here: adding one to two) and an *effect* (here: three). As a cause must always precede an effect, this means that every equation also has a *before* (here: there are two) and an *after* (here: there are three). Consequently, a mathematical equation is an *occurrence* that exists on a form of *time* continuum. In this equation, three different points can be identified on that time continuum: there are two; then another one is added to those two; now there are three. (In some equations, there can be more, potentially many more, than three points in 'time'.) Hence an equation is also a form of *sequence*.

In an equation, things need to be in their proper places. At the beginning, the one to be added must be *elsewhere* than the two. At the end, it must be with the two, to make three. At both points in time, there is a proper place for the one in relation to the two. If that proper place is not maintained, the result will be *disorder*, also known in mathematics as a wrong answer. In an equation such as this one:

$$121.9 - 79.6 = 42.3$$

...there are proper places for each of the numerals based on the quantity each is representing. The first 1 represents one hundred; the second 1 represents just 'one'. The first 9 represents nine tenths; the second 9 represents nine 'ones'. And so on. Completing this as a column subtraction would look something like this:

| 1 | 1 | 1 . | 9 |
|---|---|---|---|
| - | 7 | 9 . | 6 |
| | 4 | 2 . | 3 |

Solving the equation is a matter of maintaining *order* while carrying out a *sequence of consequences*. Individual units, tens and hundreds need to be carried one column to the right in order to perform subtraction in each column. Just like a vase bought in a shop, each item needs to be carried to its destination without being dropped, smashed,

33

forgotten, or melted down and reconstituted into something different on the way.

Arguably, mathematics is not the same thing as calculation at all. In the words of P.R. Halmos, a Professor of Mathematics at the University of Michigan, 'You can no more expect a mathematician to be able to add a column of figures rapidly and correctly than you can expect a painter to draw a straight line or a surgeon to carve a turkey—popular legend attributes such skills to these professions, but popular legend is wrong.'[25]

Rather, mathematics is a creative art, Halmos maintains. He illustrates the point using a particular mathematical problem:

*A tennis club has 1025 members and decides to hold a tournament to select a winner. Every member draws a lot to see who will play whom during the first round. The odd person left without a partner sits out. Losers are out; winners draw lots to play the next round with any extra person sitting out for that round. This routine continues until there is only one person who remains a winner.* **How many matches will have to be played?**

After presenting various computational ways in which the answer could be reached, Halmos bins them all with a flourish:

---

[25] (Halmos, 1968)

'The problem has also an inspired solution, that requires no computation, no formulas, no numbers — just pure thought. Reason like this: each match has a winner and a loser. A loser cannot participate in any later rounds; every one in the society, except only the champion, loses exactly one match. There are, therefore, exactly as many matches as there are losers, and, consequently, the number of matches is exactly one less than the membership of the society. If the number of members is 1025, the answer is 1024.'

The creative art of mathematics is the art of finding the simplest, the most elegant way of solving a problem. Mathematics is not rote learning, mnemonics or 'sick-on-the-floor' memory tricks. It is living, breathing, and therefore thinking the concepts of time, sequence and order that inexorably underpin logic and reasoning. Teach children to memorise answers, and you will create a world of people who can memorise. Show children how to think mathematically, and you will create a world blessed with able mathematicians. Why blessed? Because a world of able mathematicians is a world that is quick to solve problems and improve the conditions of life.

# Chapter 4: Arithmetic — A Hierarchy of Skills

'The time has come, the Walrus said,
To talk of many things:
Of shoes — and ships — and sealing-wax —
Of cabbages — and kings —
And why the sea is boiling hot —
And whether pigs have wings.'

Lewis Carroll,
*Through the Looking-Glass, and What Alice Found There*

Notwithstanding the lofty heights of mathematical creativity discussed in the previous chapter that transcend the world of numbers, the development of mathematical ability generally starts at the more mundane level of arithmetic — the branch of mathematics dealing with the properties and manipulation of numbers. Numbers are the ideal stomping ground for a logical discipline in which an answer is either right or wrong. Of themselves, numbers are not 'things' — they are the *idea* of a quantity as separate from actual physical objects.

This raises a problem, though. Arithmetic is taught to young children; and young children do not tend to think abstractly. Teaching children about abstract quantities without using *concrete* manipulatives to express them can make them feel about arithmetic just about the same as we feel when reading the walrus' pledge to the oysters cited at the start of this chapter.

Children who are picture thinkers are especially concrete in the way they learn. Whereas one may be able to get a neurotypical word thinker to memorise a nebulous abstraction, a picture thinker needs to 'see' the underlying concept. There is no such thing as a half-picture.

In my experience, a major contributing factor to the development of mathematical difficulties is an educational system that is too hasty to move children on from concrete quantities to abstract numerals and mathematical symbols. If you want to validate that assertion, find a person who is struggling to recall their times tables and ask them to tell you what multiplication means. It is highly unlikely that they will be able to do so. To a struggling mathematician, that little x symbol in a multiplication equation might as well signify two criss-cross sticking plasters, the place on the map where the treasure is buried, or an over-affectionate textbook author blowing an unlikely kiss.

In reality, there can be a whole number of reasons why a multiplication equation does not make sense. To multiply is to start from zero and repeatedly add the same number a certain number of times. 3 x 4 is what happens when three is added to zero once, twice, three times, then a fourth time. Multiplication is a sequence of identical additions.

It follows that a person who can multiply is a person who can add *and* who has grasped the idea of sequence. If either or both are missing or glitchy, the person will be unable to multiply. They may be able to convince the world that they can multiply — imperfectly, some of the time — by rote-learning times tables to the best of their ability. But they will not understand what they are doing, and therefore they will not know when they have made a mistake.

Assuming for a moment that an individual has acquired sufficient mathematical thinking to have grasped the idea of sequence (see previous chapter), to become a successful multiplier they will still need to have mastered addition. Mastering subtraction will also be a great help, as an agile multiplier does not always start from zero. To work out 9 x 6, for instance, you might wish to start at 10 x 6 (aka 60) and subtract 6 from that.

Addition and subtraction, however, are not finite skills. When can you say that you have mastered addition? When you can add 3 + 5, or when you can add 365,468 + 1,942,637? When you can perform the latter addition mentally, or on paper? Pragmatically, if we expect children to know their times tables up to 10 x 10 = 100, we should probably first allow them to become agile at adding and subtracting any quantities in the realm between 0 and 100.

Adding, however, is essentially learning to play leapfrog when counting forwards. To solve 12 + 3, you are counting three on from twelve, until you become good enough at it to 'skip' the 13 and the 14 and get straight to 15. Subtraction is doing the same when counting backwards. Therefore, the first step towards arithmetical competence is to learn to count, forwards and backwards.

None of the above will be news to any mathematics teacher or curriculum planner. Nobody tries to teach long division to a Reception Class. What does commonly occur, however, is this: children are moved on to the next stage in the skills hierarchy before the previous stage has been mastered.

It is easily done. From the perspective of a salaried educator with a couple of university degrees, what can be so difficult about counting? Surely all of the children in my class have mastered that? Surely we can mark that as 'done' and move on to the next item?

One might be forgiven for thinking so. Yet in my work with dyscalculia, I have frequently encountered learners —adolescents and adults included — who trip up when counting. Frequently this occurs when crossing a ten boundary — such as moving through 19, 20, 21 or 29, 30, 31 — even more frequently when counting backwards, either across a ten boundary or down through the teens. For example, a person counting down from 20 might say, '19, 18, 17, 15...'. If you move a person on to addition and subtraction before counting has become fluent and accurate, expect errors to be prolific. Moving the same learner on to multiplication and then division will be something akin to torture.

Yet counting itself has more than one layer. When a child is proudly able to 'count' out loud to a hundred, are they actually counting? Or have they simply learnt to recite a string of numerals — akin to the dyslexic child who has learnt the alphabet song but cannot find the M section in the dictionary?

Numerate counting, as opposed to mere recitation, is about conceptualising the *quantity* that each numeral represents as it is said. For this to occur, two things need to have happened: the person needs to have made a firm mental connection between each numeral and its quantity; and one quantity needs to be perceived as different from another. Perception of quantitative differences links in with the phenomenon mentioned earlier known as *subitisation*: the ability to recognise small quantities (typically up to 5) without counting them. This is sometimes referred to as *perceptual subitising*. Larger quantities can then be recognised as combinations of smaller quantities: for example, a 6 on a playing dice can be recognised as 2 groups of 3. This latter skill is sometimes called *conceptual subitising*.

Opinions differ as to whether people have maths difficulties because they have not learnt to subitise, or whether they cannot subitise because they have maths difficulties. According to the British Dyslexia Association (BDA), dyscalculia is a 'specific and persistent difficulty in understanding numbers' and is 'distinguishable from other maths issues due to the severity of difficulties with number sense, including subitising, symbolic and non-symbolic magnitude comparison, and ordering.'[26] From the BDA's perspective, therefore, dyscalculic difficulties with subitising are 'persistent', meaning they should be difficult to resolve.

I disagree. When working with dyscalculic individuals using the Davis Maths Mastery Programme, we start by making 111 balls out of white plasticine clay. In various exercises — some of which will be described later in this book — I have my dyscalculic clients lay out quantities of balls between 1 and 9. When doing so, I invite my client to think of a way that they could lay out, for example, 7 balls, in such a way that they will easily be able to recognise and visualise the quantity. Quite frequently, my clients give a great deal of thought to the layout, often breaking the larger quantity into two smaller quantities, placed side by side. For example, 9 balls might be laid out like this:

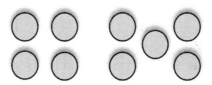

In later exercises utilising visualisation of ball quantities in adding and subtracting, my clients close their eyes and describe, with confidence and certainty, their mental 'movie' of what happens when one quantity of balls

---

[26] (British Dyslexia Association, 2023)

gets added to another. Dyscalculics *can* picture quantities; they just need to start by making a quantity in the real world, and then be allowed to choose how to arrange it.

# Chapter 5: How To Pay Attention —
# Davis Orientation Counselling

Many children with dyslexia, dyscalculia or ADHD will have got used to being told to 'pay attention!' Carl Nigi is a Davis Dyslexia Facilitator, now based in Canada but originally from my own home city of Bristol. Carl is himself dyslexic and gives a poignant account of his own experience in this regard:

'I was about 14 years old. I had been held back a year, so I was with 13-year-olds. I had been doing an intensive phonics program in the school for almost a year at this point. It involved listening to recordings of trigger words two or three a week for an hour, reading them, writing them. I look back at it now and realized it must have been a very disorienting and torturous experience.

'I do not remember the class that I was in; I do remember my teachers telling me to concentrate and pay attention on a daily, if not hourly basis!

'I remember the teacher saying, "Carl you're not concentrating, you need to pay attention!" I remember saying, "Well, you show me how you concentrate, then I'll be able to do it, the way you do it, then I'll be able to do my work, won't I!"

'It was the look of shock on her face that I remember so clearly. It was the realization that she did not know how to teach me the very thing she was insisting I should be able to do, and as she looked at me, she realized that I knew it too! It was in that moment that I understood my teachers could not help. I did not need to know the lesson that day or any other day. What I needed to know was this thing we call 'paying attention', and 'paying attention' was the very thing that none of my teachers could teach me. Looking back now, I realise that was the day I gave up in school. I spent the next year and a half staring out the window. I would become belligerent and aggressive to anybody who tried to teach me anything I did not want to learn; most of my teachers learnt to leave me alone.'

Davis Orientation Counselling is a simple, self-directed technique, devised by dyslexic author Ronald Davis, that trains children and adults to switch consciously between disorientation and orientation. Disorientation is a creative state in which the mind goes into itself in order to solve problems, daydream, or resolve confusion. Orientation is a receptive state in which the mind is present to the world around one: it sees what the eyes are seeing, hears what the ears are hearing, perceives stillness and movement accurately, and experiences time consistently. Davis Orientation Counselling provides an individual with an 'off switch' for disorientation whenever it is needed. Seen another way, it is a 'how-to' guide to paying attention.

Davis Orientation Counselling is generally administered alongside a range of other Davis techniques designed to address literacy, numeracy and/or attention focus intervention. In 2005, René Engelbrecht of Stellenbosch University, South Africa, worked with a group of 20 Afrikaans-speaking pupils in grade 5-7 from a school for learners with special needs, to study the impact of a range of Davis techniques, including Davis Orientation Counselling. Alongside gains in reading and spelling ability, Engelbrecht reports significant gains in psychological measures such as attention focus, rule-observance, behaviour, oppositional defiance, and several other emotional-behavioural categories.[27]

Solving a mathematical problem requires consistent focus; that is simply stating the obvious. Even when the problem is being solved *on* paper, it is not being solved *by* paper: the whole process is actually a series of steps that are each processed and performed mentally. First, the question needs to be fully and correctly understood. Just as I can spoil our family supper by forgetting that rice and peppers were among the things my wife asked me to get from the supermarket, so I can spoil the answer to a mathematical problem if I misunderstand or misremember key elements of the question. (This can be especially problematic when the question is a situational one — 'Tina needs to catch a bus that leaves the stop at 3:00 p.m. It takes her two minutes to put on her shoes...'

---

[27] (Engelbrecht, 2005)

etc. More about this type of problem is coming later in the book.)

Then, each step in a mathematical problem must be solved correctly. If I forget a bag of shopping at the supermarket checkout, leave the ice cream out of the fridge when unpacking, or misread 1 teaspoon of chilli powder as 1 tablespoon, the family supper is at risk once again. If I misplace or misjudge an element of an equation, my answer will be wrong.

As stated in an earlier chapter, after a period working together, I often notice my clients successfully solve a number of mathematics problems and then suddenly make an elementary mistake. One moment, 3 x 4 = 12; the next moment it is suddenly 7 or 13. Whenever performance is inconsistent — when a person can do something on one occasion but cannot do the same thing on another — the 'culprit' is usually disorientation. As well as causing perceptual distortion, disorientation can send mental processes off track, inserting a rogue mental image that deflects a process from where it was meant to be heading. During the fateful interview described at the start of Chapter 1, Diane Abbott was most probably disorientated when citing those bizarre figures. A gruelling election campaign coupled with a debilitating illness is a perfect recipe for disorientation.

When a person needs to imagine, innovate, or creatively shift their perceptions, disorientation can be very useful. When a person needs to perceive, calculate or implement accurately, it is best to be orientated. Moving appropriately between disorientation and orientation is a skill that takes practice. Davis Orientation Counselling gives a person a tool to do this; the use of the tool then needs to be habituated. In a Davis Programme, this is normally done over an intensive block of one-to-one learning sessions, after which the individual starts to apply the tool independently in everyday life.

Humans are humans. Even an experienced Davis veteran remains prone to the occasional spontaneous disorientation. Twenty years after receiving my own Davis Programme, I can still forget where I put my keys. But after living three pre-Davis decades with a terrible aim, I now often win at darts, bowling and minigolf. I can still lose focus without immediately realising it; but when I need to be in focus, I have a simple and reliable tool for getting there.

The Davis Orientation Counselling Procedure is described in detail in Ronald Davis' books, *The Gift of Dyslexia* and *The Gift of Learning*. In both books, full instructions are provided for implementing the procedure. For those who struggle with mathematics, Davis Orientation Counselling is a game-changer. Once such a person has an orientation tool, they can control their focus. Once they can control their focus, they can start a new learning journey around mathematics. And then, when solving mathematical problems, they can start, not just to find the right answer, but to know when they have done so.

# Chapter 6: The Gift of Mastery

According to Ronald Davis, the gift of dyslexia is the gift of mastery. When it comes to learning, mastery is the polar opposite of rote learning, memorisation, and 'cramming'.

Mastery is rich, experiential learning that utilises the learner's own creativity. Mastery is not being told something and trying to remember it; mastery is actively re-creating the thing that is being learnt, usually in the physical world, putting something of you into the process. Too often, traditional learning resorts to passive methods that try to 'stick' new knowledge onto an individual. Stick something on, and it can come unstuck again. By contrast, when something is mastered, the learner's own act of re-creation allows the new knowledge or skill to grow out of who the learner already is. In Davis' own words:

'When someone masters something, it becomes part of that person. It becomes part of the individual's thought and creative process. It adds the quality of its essence to all subsequent thought and creativity of the individual.'[28]

If you have learnt to drive a car, you will know the difference between learning and mastery. You will recall

---

[28] (Davis & Braun, 2010)

the time when you were receiving instruction and had to think about every individual action you needed to take. Mirror, signal, manoeuvre, footbrake, clutch, gears – remember? The intensity of thought involved could leave a person feeling quite tense and tired.

Yet once you have passed your test and have been driving for a while, these functions become pretty much automatic. You may even be able to daydream, listen to the radio or hold conversations while performing them.

When all the component skills of a new skill have been not just learnt, but mastered, acquiring the next level of skill becomes easy. People who experience the Davis methods often wonder at how easily and quickly new skills can be acquired that have challenged a person for years before.

Mastery is at least as important for dyscalculics as for dyslexics. As discussed earlier, people with mathematical challenges tend to be creative, picture-thinking, hands-on learners who readily shift their perceptions using the mechanism known in the Davis methods as disorientation. Just like dyslexics, they learn best, not just through concrete manipulatives, but through something that they have made themselves.

Four decades ago, Ronald Davis discovered the power of plasticine clay as a learning medium for dyslexics that allows mastery to occur naturally. Using clay, Davis guides dyslexic individuals to make the symbols, words and concepts that have hitherto confused them. The act of creation replaces confusion with certainty and ownership.

Later, Davis devised a similar set of procedures for learners who struggle with mathematics. Here too, people who have struggled all their lives with mathematical concepts and processes are able to become confident and fluent in them, quickly.

Mrs T. (Rory's maths teacher) was hugely complimentary about your work with Rory (and quite emotional about his CE result!) today, as was his science teacher who noted the dramatic improvement in Rory's ability after your sessions. Rory is the only non-scholarship student to win the headmaster's academic endeavour award! Your ears must be constantly burning with the amount of times I sing your praises to everyone!

Before attending your 'Davis' sessions, G. could not 'see' how mathematical problems could be solved. She had been struggling with Maths back in year 3 and after being assessed by an educational psychologist we realised that she had Dyscalculia. Her school continued to teach her in the same way and she struggled along. As her parents we were keen to seek some further help for her and took her to additional maths on a Saturday morning. Whilst this certainly helped, we kept looking for alternatives and discovered the Davis technique. From this we sought a teacher and found you.

At first we were sceptical as to how there could be a link to clay modelling and solving maths. At the end of the sessions, however, I am convinced that this has had the single most significant benefit to G.'s learning of both maths and other subjects. The combinations of the technique and the patient delivery removed her fear of maths and showed how it could be done.

What you gave her was the ability to 'see' maths and lose the fear of it.

'The Davis Maths Mastery course matched the pace my child needed to learn. I witnessed my son grasp concepts with speed and clarity, growing in confidence and excitement to learn more. Maths very quickly became his favourite subject.

'We were both blown away by how quickly years of lost learning were set in a foundation which became easy to build upon.'

He can't remember the time he did not understand Maths.'

# Chapter 7: Mastering Mathematical Thinking — Davis Concept Mastery

As discussed in Chapter 3, a person needs to be able to think mathematically before they can solve mathematical problems correctly and know that they have done so. In a Davis Maths Mastery Programme, prior to embarking on any mathematical operations, the participant is taken through a process known as Davis Concept Mastery: a creative learning module, anchored in models made by the participant out of plasticine clay, that enables the following concepts to be fully assimilated into the individual's identity. The process revolves around the following principal concepts:

| | |
|---|---|
| change | something becoming something else |
| consequence | something that happens as a result of something else (subdivided into *cause* and *effect*, *before* and *after*) |
| time | the measurement of change in relation to a standard |
| sequence | the way things follow each other, one after another |
| order | things in their proper places, proper positions, and proper conditions |
| disorder | things not in their proper places, and/or not in their proper positions, and/or not in their proper conditions[29] |

---

[29] The Gift of Learning

All of the concepts mastered are rooted in the concept of self, depicted as a clay figure representing the participant that is present in every concept model.

The meaning of each concept is discussed and briefly investigated in the environment; the discussion and exploration is rooted in a simple definition of the concept, known as its principle. Based on the discussion and investigation, the participant makes their own creative depiction of the concept, using white plasticine clay to create the model and the word.

*Fig. 3: a participant's depiction of* consequence: something that happens as a result of something else. *Subsequently, the left hand side of the model can be identified as* cause *and the right-hand side as* effect. *Then, the left-hand side can be identified as* before *and the right-hand side as* after.

After all the concepts have been mastered in this way, the participant has created their own frame of reference for understanding the meaning and logic behind any mathematical problem. The participant can begin to *think mathematically*. During subsequent work with arithmetic, the concepts mastered are referenced conversationally in a number of ways, as will be shown in the following chapters.

Towards the end of the programme, after the participant has comprehensively explored and mastered all basic arithmetical functions, the clay is used once again to link the principles of arithmetic back to the concepts previously mastered. A simple equation is made in which real quantities — clay balls — are used instead of numerals. The participant then reconstructs each concept model and finds the concept in the equation.

*Fig. 4: a participant's depiction of* effect: *something that is made to happen.*
*In the creative model, a flower is made to happen (by the participant planting a seed). In the equation model, 3 is made to happen (by adding 2 to 1). Photo: Margot Young.*

For many participants, mastering the concept of *time* can open a whole new chapter in their lives. As mentioned previously, I am yet to meet a dyscalculic individual who did not struggle with the concept of time. Davis Concept Mastery provides an opportunity for rich explorations of time that enable a participant to finally 'see' what time is.

Here is an outline, in note form, of how I work with many clients on the concept of time. Note: this is an excerpt from the longer Davis Concept Mastery process; it is shown here as an example of how this process might look in a session. For full effectiveness, a learner will need to go through the full process, either with a licensed Davis

Programme Facilitator or with a family member who has received workshop training from their regional Davis office.

| What to do | What to say |
|---|---|
| *Roll out a short length of clay.* | Here is a rope made of clay. How would you measure *how* long it is? |
| *If the answer 'a ruler' or 'a tape measure' is not forthcoming, supply this information. Get out a real classroom ruler. As required, guide your learner towards laying the rope alongside the ruler.* | |
| *Briefly discuss the units of length shown on the ruler.* | Look at the markings on the ruler. Do you know what they are called? |
| | Would the ruler work if it were made of elastic? Why not? |

## *Units of measurement*

| What to do | What to say |
|---|---|
| *On the ruler, have the learner count how many millimetres there are in a centimetre. Establish that there are 10 millimetres in every centimetre.* | |
| *Say:* | Therefore, millimetres and centimetres are part of the same system of measurement. We call them *units of measurement.* |
| *Establish that we usually choose the unit most convenient for the size of what we are measuring. If appropriate for the learner's age and maturity, discuss metres and kilometres as units for measuring longer lengths and distances.* | Would it be convenient to measure your height in millimetres? Why not? What about the distance from here to your home? |

## *Introduction to standards*

| What to do | What to say |
|---|---|
| *All the units so far discussed originate from the metre standard. The origin of the metre standard as one ten millionth of the distance from the North Pole to the Equator can be of great interest to some learners. Sources of this information are readily available on the Internet; you and your learner could potentially investigate them together.* | |
| *If your learner expresses interest, you can also explore how other standards were derived from the metre standard (one gram is the mass of one cubic centimetre of water; one litre is the space occupied by 1,000 cubic centimetres of water).* | |

| | |
|---|---|
| *Caution: do not over-provide information here. Intuit your learner's level of interest, and be guided by it.* | |
| *Establish that your learner understands that you cannot measure one phenomenon (e.g. mass) with a unit of measurement expressing another phenomenon (e.g. length).* | Could you measure your mass/weight in metres? Why not? |

## Measurement of change: the day standard

| What to do | What to say |
|---|---|
| *Have your learner think of a simple example of a change that would take less than a day to complete. (E.g. baking a loaf of bread). Have your learner make a model of the change out of plasticine. The model should show a 'before' and an 'after' that are connected with an arrow.* | |

| | |
|---|---|
| *A human figure denoting the learner themselves should be either observing the change or involved in making the change happen.* | |
|  Fig. 5: An example of a model for 'change'. *A new piece of paper becomes a scrunched-up piece of paper. The participant's model of themselves is standing and observing the change.* | |
| *Discuss how we measure change.* | What instrument(s) would we use to measure this change? |
| *If your learner does not immediately understand, rephrase and ask:* | What instrument(s) would we use to measure how long this change takes? |
| *In response, your learner should name a timepiece such as a clock/watch/stopwatch.* | |

| | |
|---|---|
| *Have your learner make two copies of a timepiece out of clay. Have your learner place one copy at the 'before' end of the change and one at the 'after' end.* | |

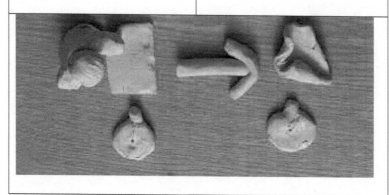

## Units and standard of change measurement

| What to do | What to say |
|---|---|
| | What units do we find on a [timepiece previously named by the learner]? |
| *Discuss how seconds fit exactly into minutes (x 60) and minutes into hours (x 60).* | |

| | |
|---|---|
| *Your learner should respond: 'a day'. If not, supply the information and discuss.* | What unit is the next one up? What do hours fit exactly into? |

## The day standard

| What to do | What to say |
|---|---|
| *Discuss how the times of day reflect the real processes of day and night.* | Would it be a good idea to go for a picnic at midnight? Why not? |
| *Elicit the response from your learner: 'It is dark'.* | |
| | Is it always dark at midnight? |
| *Your learner should respond 'yes'. But does your learner know why? As needed, proceed to explore the answer with a globe and torch (see next section).* | |

## *The day standard: globe-and-torch demonstration*

*Note: even better than a torch is a modern round table lamp or orb, if available.*

| What to do | What to say |
|---|---|
| *Place a small piece of plasticine on the globe, on the place where the session with your learner is taking place (e.g. on the south-eastern part of Great Britain if the session is taking place in London).* | |
| *Darken the room.* | |
| *Have your learner switch on the torch and point it directly at one side of the globe. The torch represents the sun.* | |
| *Discuss with your learner which direction on the globe is east.* | |
| *Discuss with your learner that, first thing in the morning, we see the sun in the east of the sky.* | This is called 'sunrise'. |

| | |
|---|---|
| *Instruct your learner to turn the globe to show the earth's position when it is sunrise in the place marked by the piece of plasticine.* | |
| | Can you now work out which way the earth spins? |
| *Give assistance as needed.* | |
| *Have your learner turn the globe (in the 'right' direction) and explore how the earth is positioned in relation to the sun when, at the place marked with plasticine, it is:*<br><br>o  *midday;*<br>o  *mid-afternoon;*<br>o  *early evening / sunset;*<br>o  *midnight;*<br>o  *etc.* | |
| *When this has been thoroughly explored, ask:* | How long does it take for the earth to make one full rotation? |

| | |
|---|---|
| *Assist with further discussion as needed.* | |
| | What do you think: does the earth speed up and slow down as it turns, or does it go at a more or less constant speed? |
| | Why is this important in order that the earth's rotation can serve as a time standard? |
| *If appropriate, discuss again why a ruler would not work if it were made of elastic (see above). Compare this (hypothetically) to an earth which changed speed as it turned.* | |
| *If your learner is well-travelled, and/or has relatives elsewhere in the world, and seems interested, you could explore time zones. E.g. what time of day (roughly) is it in New York when it is early evening in the UK?* | |

*Have your learner make a large round ball out of plasticine clay and place it behind the model depicting a change. This represents the earth. Have the learner fashion a curved arrow out of clay and place it around the edge of the ball, to show that the earth rotates on its axis.*

*Fig. 6: an example of a model for time.*
*The change from new piece of paper to scrunched-up piece is being measured using a stopwatch, in seconds. A second is 1/86400 of the time it takes for the earth to complete a full rotation on its axis (the standard of measurement).*

This process led the mother of one 11-year-old boy whom I worked with to tell me that I had ruined the family holiday. Right after our session on *time*, the family went abroad for a short break. Whereas in the past, the boy would have been simply 'in the now', with no sense of time until the day of departure arrived, now he was running a mental countdown clock — 'Mum, we've only got three days left; Mum, we've only got two days left; Mum, we're leaving in six hours!' When I next saw the boy, he got hold of my globe and lamp and enthusiastically showed me the position of the earth when the family had left for the airport at 3am, its position when they had taken off at 7am, and so on. For the boy's mother, I think the negative effect on the family holiday was mitigated by the fact that he had grasped time in a way that he never had done before.

At this point, time has been mastered in the context of a change that occurs within a day, the measurement of such a change using a timepiece (clock/watch/stopwatch etc), and the standard that governs the workings of all clocks (the earth's rotation on its axis). The learner then needs to explore, model and master time in the context of longer-term changes. These are generally measured using calendars; and calendars are governed by the earth's orbit around the sun. A full orbit takes one year.

With many of my Davis clients, alongside the clay modelling process and other explorations, I conduct a demonstration with a globe and a lamp to explore: first, how the earth's rotation creates night and day; and secondly, how the earth's orbit around the sun creates the seasons.

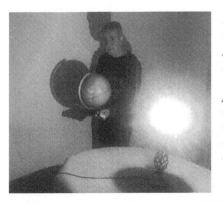

*Fig 7: exploring the earth's orbit around the sun with a globe and a lamp.*
*By keeping the globe at a tilt as it is moved round the lamp, it is possible to explore how the earth's position and movement creates the seasons. A full orbit around the sun can then be seen as the definition of a year.*

Once this principle has been fully understood, the learner makes a second model of time, this time featuring a change that takes longer than a day, a calendar at the before and the after, and a depiction of the earth orbiting the sun while also rotating on its own axis.

*Fig 8: a model for time where the change being measured takes more than a day to complete.*
*The change from seeds into plants is measured using a calendar. Every date on the calendar is a position on the earth's annual orbit around the sun (the standard of measurement).*

On an individual basis, this process can open up possibilities for further explorations of how time works. For a sample script outlining how I have taught dyscalculic learners to tell the time from an analogue clock, see my first book, *Why Tyrannosaurus But Not If?*

One 13-year-old girl, whom we shall call Cindy, took a Davis Maths Mastery Programme with me a number of years ago. At an initial meeting before the programme, she complained that she struggled to remember the months of the year. Towards the end of the programme, we found ourselves with a couple of spare hours in the schedule, so we decided to explore this.

We went into the largest room in the office, where we had a large table usually used for training workshops. First, Cindy made a large clay ball to represent the sun and placed it in the middle of the table. Then, she made 12 smaller balls, each representing the earth at a different point on its orbit around the sun. She carved a line into each ball to represent the equator. Then she placed a small piece of clay at each of the 'poles'. Finally, she poked a small hole in each ball in the approximate location of the United Kingdom (where the programme was taking place).

We then agreed that, whenever she placed an 'earth' somewhere on the orbit around the sun, the North Pole would always tilt towards the wall where the door was that led back to our session room. This corresponded with the real Earth's North Pole always tilting towards Polaris — the North Star.

She then placed one of the 'earths' between the 'sun' and the 'north star' wall. She ensured that the 'north pole' of the clay ball was tilted away from the 'sun', towards the wall. Earlier, when mastering the concept of time, we had discussed and explored in depth the connection between the Earth's position on its solar orbit and the seasons. Now, we recalled that exploration and concluded that the ball just placed on the table represented the earth in December, at the time of the northern hemisphere's winter solstice. She made the word *December* out of clay and placed it in front of the ball.

She then placed another of the 'earths' on the opposite side of the sun, with the north tilted towards the sun. We discussed why this shows the northern hemisphere's summer solstice and depicts the earth's position on its solar orbit in June. She made the word June and placed it in front of the model.

She then repeated the same process, placing an 'earth' in the correct position at each of the two equinoxes and making the words September and March.

Then she added in the remaining earths, one for each remaining month, adding the name of each month in clay.

*Fig. 9: my client's complete model of the months of the year, each shown as a position of the earth on its orbit around the sun.*

Next, she looked at each model, touched it, and stated the name of the month, in forwards order from January to December. She then did the same thing in backwards order from December to January.

Finally, she closed her eyes and named the months forwards and backwards in the correct order, from her mental image.

Eight years later, I received a message on LinkedIn from Cindy's uncle, thanking me for the progress that Cindy's cousin had made after his own Davis Programme with me. I thanked him for his kind message and asked how Cindy was getting on. It turned out that she was in her final year at the London School of Economics. Not bad at all for a girl who at the start of her teens could not order the months of the year.

To experience the power of the Davis Concept Mastery process in full, see The Gift of Learning by Ronald Davis, contact your regional Davis office to learn this process in a live training workshop, or contact a licensed Davis Programme Facilitator for a personal programme.

## Chapter 8: First Steps in Arithmetic — Counting and Place Value

In the previous chapter, we examined how the concepts of change, consequence, time, sequence, and the difference between order and disorder need to be fully mastered before any attempt is made to learn mathematics. Mastering these concepts enables a person to think mathematically. Only when this has occurred can a person start to explore mathematical operations.

As discussed earlier, the act of counting underlies all arithmetical operations. If you cannot count forwards, you cannot add. If you cannot count backwards, you cannot subtract. If you cannot add and subtract, you cannot multiply or divide. If you cannot divide, you cannot compute fractions, decimals or percentages. Therefore — at the risk of stating the obvious — mathematical learning must start with counting.

One should not assume that a mathematically challenged person can count. They may be able to recite the numerals from 1 to 10, or even from 1 to 100, but that is not the same as counting. Counting is about processing a sequence in amount — a quantity that increases or decreases by 1 at each step. It is perfectly possible to learn to recite from 1 to 100 without being aware, for instance, that 9 is one more than 8, or that 16 is one less than 17.

Building this awareness, richly and fully, will make a person fluent in counting, both forwards and backwards. Here is an example of how this is approached in a Davis Maths Mastery Programme. Notice how the concepts of order and disorder, which are mastered using the Davis Concept Mastery procedure at an earlier stage of the programme (see Chapter 6), are referenced repeatedly here:

| | |
|---|---|
| **Note:** *If possible, sit opposite your learner for this and all subsequent exercises. Seeing your learner's face will help you pick up, and respond to, any facial signs of confusion.* | |

| DO or OBSERVE: | SAY: |
|---|---|
| *Make a numeral 2 from clay and* **Ask** | Do you know what this is? |
| *If your learner answers 'two' or 'the number two,' place two balls in front of your learner, and* **Say** | No, this is two. |
| *Place the numeral so it is above the two balls for your learner, and* **Say** | This is the **numeral** 2. It is a symbol that represents the number two or the quantity two. |

| | |
|---|---|
| *Pointing to the two balls first, and then the numeral,* **Say** | The **number** and the **numeral** have the same name. The numeral is just a symbol that represents the number or quantity. |
| **Ask** | Does that make sense to you? |
| *If 'yes,' go on; if 'no,' continue the explanation.* | |
| *Have your learner make the numerals 1 through 9 and place them in a row on the table.*<br><br>*Point to the 1, and* **Ask** | How many does this numeral represent? |
| *When answered,* **Say** | Show me the number. |
| *Have your learner put the ball above the numeral.* | |
| *Follow the same model with the two, three, four, and five.* **Ask** | Could you do this for all the numerals to one hundred? |
| *If yes, go on. If no, continue until the answer is yes, and then go on.* | |

| | | |
|---|---|---|
| *Point to a place on the table where there is no clay, and* **Ask** | | How many? |
| *When answered,* **Ask** | | Do you know the numeral for zero? |
| *If no, demonstrate it for them. Have your learner make a zero and place it before the numeral one.* | | |
| | **Say** | 'The zero is very important because without it we cannot do maths with a pencil. The idea of zero is, there is nothing there, and that is a very important idea. |

*Have your learner master the numerals 0 – 9, together with the numbers they represent, along the following lines:*

- *Progressing from 0 through to 9, have your learner look at each numeral and the quantity of balls above it. Have them name the number while touching the numeral and the balls*
- *Have your learner do the same as above, but in reverse — from 9 through do 0*
- *Have your learner repeat each of the above two steps, but this time looking and naming without touching*
- *Have your learner close their eyes and name the numbers from 0 to 9, from their mental image of what was created. Note: if any of the mental pictures of the numerals and/or quantities are unclear, have your learner peek, then close their eyes again and continue*

> - *Have your learner do the same as in the previous step, but in reverse — from 9 through to 0*
>
> *Note: If significant signs of confusion occur, you are likely to need the assistance of a Davis Facilitator and/or attend workshop training with your regional Davis office to learn how this can be resolved.*

A learner who can complete the above steps with certainty is now able to count fluently up and down between 0 and 9. The next step is to explore how quantities greater than 9 are arranged and symbolically depicted in mathematics. This is known as *place value* in the *base ten system*:

---

*Have your learner clear away all the numerals and numbers except for 9. Have your learner move the numeral and number 9 to a space a little to the right of the centre of the table, directly in front of your learner. The balls showing the number 9 should still be directly above the numeral 9.*

| *Point to the 9 balls, and* | |
|---|---|
| ***Say:*** | This is the largest quantity that can be represented by a single numeral symbol. Does that make sense? |
| *Playfully toss a 10th ball in amidst the 9 balls and.* ***Say:*** | We have a problem; I have created disorder. With the numerals we have, we can't create order here (point to the place the numeral 9 is) |

|  | because we don't have a numeral symbol that can represent this quantity (point to the place where the 10 balls are). So we need to assign a new order. |
|---|---|
| *Giving as much guidance as is needed, have your learner create a cluster of 10 balls consisting of a base made out of 6 balls (arranged 3 x 2) and a top made out of 4 balls (2 x 2).* |  |
| *Point to a space a little to your learner's left from the 9 and the cluster. Let your learner leave the 9 numeral in place for now.* **Say:** | Move this cluster of 10 balls to here. |
| *Make another 10-cluster. Place it, and a single clay ball, in your area of the table. (You will need these as demonstration props.)* |  |
| *Point to the place where your learner's 10-cluster has been put.* **Say:** | We can now create *order*. This is the place where |

| | |
|---|---|
| | we will count these (*pick up your 10-cluster and show it to your learner*). Not individual '1's (*show your learner your single clay ball*), but these (*show your learner your 10-cluster*). |
| **Note:** *If appropriate, you could introduce the term 'units' here instead of '1's.* | |
| *Point to the empty space above the numeral 9, where the 9 balls had previously been.* **Say:** | This is still the place where we count these (*pick up your single ball and show it to your learner*). |
| **Say:** | So let's create order with the numerals now. This (*point to the numeral 9*) is disorder, isn't it? What numeral do you need to place here instead, to show how many '1's there are here? |
| *Your learner should remove the numeral 9 and put the numeral 0 in its place.* | |
| **Say:** | That is correct. And what numeral do you need to place here (*point to the space below the 10-* |

| | |
|---|---|
| | *cluster*), to show how many of these (*point to the 10-cluster*) there are here? Not how many individual '1's; how many of these (*point again to the 10-cluster*). |
| *Your learner should place the numeral 1 below the 10-cluster.* | |
| *Sweep your hand across both figures of the numeral 10 and* **Ask:** | Do you know what this numeral is called? |
| *As needed, guide your learner to the answer 'ten'. Then* **Say:** | So this is why we write 10 as a '1' and a '0': the numerals are showing that there is one of these (point to the 10-cluster) and no individual '1's. |
| *Write '11' on a piece of paper. Show it to your learner.* **Ask:** | How would you show '11' in the same way? |
| *Your learner should leave the 10-cluster and the numeral 1 in the tens' place, remove the numeral 0 from the units' place, add a ball in the units area and* | |

| | |
|---|---|
| *place the numeral 1 above it.* | |
| *When done,* **Say:** | That is correct. |
| *Repeat this process with further numbers and numerals between 12 and 99. Do as many examples as needed until your learner can confidently show the quantity and numeral in each case.* | |
| *Write '99' on a piece of paper.* **Say:** | Make 99 in the same way. I can help you if you like. |
| *If you do help to make the clusters, keep back the 10-cluster and the individual ball you placed on your side of the table earlier.* | |
| *When your learner has made 99 – the numerals and the number – playfully toss an extra ball in amidst the 9 units.* **Then Say:** | I have created disorder. Can you create order? |
| *Your learner should form a 10-cluster out of the 10 balls and move it to the place where the 9 existing 10-clusters are arranged. Your learner may well* | |

| | |
|---|---|
| *notice the problem with this.* | |
| *Whether or not the problem is noticed,* **Say:** | Now there is disorder in the 10s' area, because you have ten 10-clusters and we don't have a numeral symbol to show any quantity greater than 9. So how can you create order? |
| *See if your learner can work out that they need to cluster all the 10-clusters together into a 100-cluster and move it one space to their left. Give guidance as needed. Let your learner leave the numerals '99' in place for now.* | |
| *When this is done,* **Say:** | Now make order with the numerals. This is the place where you count these (point to the 100-cluster). How many of these do you have here? |
| *Elicit the answer '1', then* **Say:** | Place the numeral here (*point to the space below the 100-cluster*) that shows this. |
| | This is the place where you count these (*point to* |

| | |
|---|---|
| | *your 10-cluster that you made earlier*). How many of these are there here? (*Point to the empty space above the '9' numeral in the tens column.*) |
| *Elicit the answer 'zero' / 'nought' / 'none'. Guide your learner to replace the numeral 9 with the numeral 0.* | |
| ***Say:*** | This is the place where you count these (*point to the single ball on your side of the table*). How many of these are there here? (*Point to the empty space above the '9' numeral in the units column.*) |
| *Elicit the answer 'zero' / 'nought' / 'none'. Guide your learner to replace the numeral 9 with the numeral 0.* | |
| *Your learner has now created the numeral 100. As appropriate,* ***Say:*** | That is how we write one hundred as a numeral. |
| ***Say:*** | Now show one hundred and eleven in the same way, as a number and numeral. |

| *Give your learner guidance as needed.* | |
|---|---|

If appropriate to your learner's maturity and interest, the following step could be added:

| |
|---|
| *Have your learner remove the numerals 111 but leave the quantities in place. Invite them to imagine what the following quantities would look like:*<br>• *222*<br>• *999*<br><br>*Then ask your learner if they can visualise what would happen if one ball were added to 999. Have your learner talk you through his 'mental movie' of the steps that would be involved to create order, ending with a 1000 cluster in the 1000s' column.* |
| *Briefly discuss what a 10,000 and a 100,000 cluster would look like.* |

# Chapter 9: The Next Layer — Mental Addition

Once a person has mastered counting and the principles of base ten place value, they can proceed to explore and master addition. As mentioned earlier, addition is essentially 'leapfrog counting'. Adding 3 to 15 is the same as counting from 15 to 18, but skipping the 16 and the 17.

Are we talking about written arithmetic or mental arithmetic here? Actually, the distinction is an artificial one. As discussed earlier, written arithmetic is simply a series of steps of mental arithmetic, each of which is recorded on paper in the correct place and in the correct manner. Therefore, to build arithmetic proficiency, one must always start with the mental processes.

The prize we are seeking here is fluency and accuracy in mental addition. To cite the title of this book — when this is achieved, counting on fingers becomes a thing of the past. If, later, the person wants to master the multiplication tables as far as 10 x 10, being able to add mentally up to a total of 100 will be a very useful asset. That is because, as we shall see later, multiplication is essentially a process of repeated adding.

The first step is to have a clear mental image of what adding is, conceptually. A simple definition of *add* could be *to put one amount with another amount.* Adding is a type of *change* and, therefore, *consequence*: concepts which, in a Davis Maths Mastery Programme, will have been mastered in clay before any work on arithmetic is embarked upon.

The following script, based on the Davis Maths Mastery Approach, is an example of how I help my clients to achieve fluency in mental addition. Once again, notice how the concepts of *order* and *disorder* are referenced:

| DO or OBSERVE: | SAY: |
|---|---|
| *From clay fashion an equal sign, and* **Ask** | Do you know what this is? |
| *If there is any hesitation in the answer, explain and demonstrate it, then have your learner explain and demonstrate to you.* | |
| *Next, your learner would go through the Symbol Mastery steps, with the equal sign and the word* **equal**. *See The Gift of Dyslexia by Ronald Davis for the Davis Symbol Mastery Procedure steps.*<br><br>*When doing Symbol Mastery with maths function symbols, the clay models should have:* | |

| | |
|---|---|
| • a 'real world' model<br><br>• the function symbol in an 'equation' using clay balls<br><br>• the word being mastered. | |
| Make a plus sign (+), then<br><br>**Ask** | Do you know what this is? |
| If there is any hesitation in the answer, explain and demonstrate it, then have your learner explain and demonstrate to you. | |
| Next, your learner would go through the Symbol Mastery steps, with the plus sign and the word **add**. See The Gift of Dyslexia by Ronald Davis for the Davis Symbol Mastery Procedure steps.<br><br>Have your learner remove the word **add** and re-master the model and plus sign with the word **plus**.<br><br>Have your learner remove everything that has been made. | |
| Set up two long ropes in a cross shape. | |

| | |
|---|---|
| *The cross shape creates four quadrants on the table. Discuss with your learner how each of these four quadrants will be used.* **Say:**  | We now need to agree on an order. This (*sweep your hand over the two quadrants on your learner's left*) is the proper place for tens. This (*sweep your hand over the two quadrants on your learner's right*) is the proper place for ones. |
| **Say:** | When one number is going to be added to another, the proper place for the first number is here (*sweep your hand over the two quadrants furthest from your learner*). The proper place for the number that you are going to add in is here (*sweep your hand over the two quadrants closest to your learner*). |
| *On a piece of paper, write 11 + 12. Show this to your learner.* | |
| | Up at the top (*sweep your* |

| | |
|---|---|
| *Instruct your learner how to place these numbers in the quadrants.* **Say:** 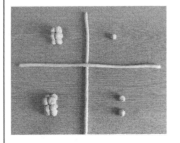 | *hand over the two quadrants nearest to you),* place a ten cluster on this side (*point to the quadrant that is top left for your learner*) and one ball on this side (*point to the quadrant that is top right for your learner*).<br><br>Down at the bottom (*sweep your hand over the two quadrants nearest to your learner*), place a ten cluster on this side (*point to the quadrant that is bottom left for your learner*) and two balls on this side (*point to the quadrant that is bottom right for your learner*). |
| *Show your learner how to perform the addition with the numbers in the quadrants.* **Say:** | The two single balls from the bottom are brought up to the top.<br><br>The ten cluster from the bottom is brought up to the top. |
| *In the top quadrants, there should now be two tens and three ones.* |  |

| | *Ask:* | How many? |
|---|---|---|
| *Elicit the answer: 23.*<br><br>*On the piece of paper showing 11 + 12, write an = sign. Pass the paper and a pencil to your learner, and*     *Ask:* | | Would you like to write the answer after the equal sign? |
| *On a piece of paper, write 33 + 21.*     *Say:* | | Now show me 33 + 21. |
| *On the left hand side, there will be 3 ten clusters on top and 2 ten clusters on the bottom.*<br><br>*On the right hand side, there will be 3 balls on top and 1 ball on the bottom.* | | |
| *Have your learner solve the addition in the same way as in the previous example. When done, write an = sign after 33 + 21. Pass the paper and a pencil to your learner and invite them to write down the answer.* | | |
| *Continue in the same way with further addition problems until your learner is solving such examples fluently and* | | |

| | |
|---|---|
| *confidently and recognises he is doing so. At this stage, avoid addition problems that require carrying (exchanging).* | |
| *Once your learner is solving the examples fluently,* **Say:** | When you don't have clay to hand and need to solve an addition of this kind, you can do so in just the same way, but using your imagination. Are you ready to try? |
| *If your learner says 'No,' continue with further examples as practised above. Once your learner responds 'Yes,' proceed to the next step.* | |
| *On a piece of paper, re-write the last addition problem that was demonstrated by your learner in clay,* **without the answer.** *Have your learner set up the problem in clay,* **without proceeding to the answer.** | |
| **Say:** | Close your eyes and picture what you did in |

| | |
|---|---|
| | the clay to solve the problem. If you picture it clearly, talk me through it. If it doesn't come clearly, open your eyes and redo it in the clay for real, then tell me the answer. |
| *Once your learner has given you the correct answer with certainty, write an equal sign after the addition problem and invite the client to write the answer.* | |
| *Continue in the same way with further addition problems. Continue to avoid addition problems that require carrying (exchanging). When your learner is confidently solving addition problems using mental imagery, move on.* | |
| *On a piece of paper, write 13 + 18. Show this to your learner. Instruct your learner to lay out this problem in the quadrants and to commence solving it.* ***Say:*** | Show me this problem on |

| | |
|---|---|
| | the quadrants. How would you solve this one? |
| *As your learner starts to solve the problem on the grid, they should recognise that adding the two numbers creates disorder in the top right (units') quadrant. Discuss this in as much detail as is needed.* | |
| ***Say:*** | We now have disorder here (point to the the top right quadrant) because we don't have a numeral to represent this quantity. Do you know how to establish order here? |
| *Instructing as needed, have your learner form a cluster out of 10 of the balls in their top right (units) quadrant and carry it over to their top left (tens) quadrant.* | |
| *Instructing as needed, have your learner complete the addition by moving the 10-cluster in their bottom left quadrant up to their top left quadrant. When done, write an = sign after 13 + 18. Pass the paper and a* | |

| | |
|---|---|
| *pencil to your learner, and* **Say:** | Would you like to write the answer after the equal sign? |
| *Continue in the same way with further addition examples that require carrying (exchanging), until your learner is solving such examples fluently and confidently and recognises they are doing so.* | |
| **Say:** | Just as with the earlier problems you solved, you will be able to do this using your imagination if we put in one further piece. |
| **Say:** | The problem with this type of addition is that there is a moment when you have to create temporary disorder in the place where you are collecting the units (*point to the quadrant that is top right for your learner*). When this happens, there can be as many as 18 balls in that place, and that can be difficult to visualise. But by putting in an extra |

| | |
|---|---|
| | piece, we can make this easy. |
| *Pass a 10-cluster to your learner. Instruct your learner to separate the cluster into individual balls and lay them out in a column, well off to the side from the addition quadrants but within your learner's working area.*<br><br>***Ask:*** | How many in this line? |
| *(Your learner should confidently answer, 'Ten,' because he created the line out of a 10-cluster.)* | |
| *Have your learner roll out a short length of clay about 1 inch / 3cm long.* | |
| *Point to the line of 10 balls and*<br>***Say:*** | Let's call this a *line of ten*. Using this line of ten and this rope (*point to the short length of clay*), we can see any two amounts that add together to make 10. |
| *Have your learner place the rope between the two balls furthest away from him in the line of ten, i.e. between the 9th and 10th* | |

| | |
|---|---|
| *balls. Sweep your hand over the single ball above the rope and* **Ask:** | How many here? |
| *Elicit the answer: 'One.'* | |
| *Sweep your hand over the 9 balls below and* **Ask:** | How many here? |
| *Elicit the answer: 'Nine.'* | |
| **Say:** | So one plus nine equals ten, right? |
| *Get your learner's agreement. Establish certainty before moving on.* | |
| *Move the rope one step down and place it between the 8th and 9th balls. Repeat the same procedure and questioning as before, always starting with the quantity further from your learner. Establish certainty before moving on, intermittently asking 'Are you sure?' and 'Prove it.'* | |
| *Continue the same procedure and questioning, moving the rope down one place each time until the quantities 10 and 0 are reached. At each* | |

| | |
|---|---|
| *step, establish certainty before moving on.* | |
| *Next, go through the process in reverse by moving the rope up one place each time. As before, always start with the quantity further from your learner. Continue until the quantities 0 and 10 are reached. At each step, establish certainty before moving on.* | |
| *When done, place the rope in random positions in the line of ten, questioning as before. Continue with random placements, questioning each time, until all possible combinations have been explored and your learner is experiencing confidence.* | |
| *When done, leave the line of ten intact, with the rope placed nearby.* | |
| *With your learner, return to the addition quadrants. On a piece of paper, write 29 + 33. Show this to your learner and* **Say:** | |

|  |  |
|---|---|
|  | Lay this one out in the quadrants. |
| *Once the problem has been laid out,* **Say:** | While you solve this one, let's talk it through step by step. What is the first step? |
| *Elicit from your learner that the 3 balls in your learner's bottom right quadrant are to be moved up to the top right quadrant.* |  |
| **Say:** | OK, go ahead and move the 3 balls to the top quadrant, but this time, set them apart from the 9 balls that are already there. |
| *Allow your learner to perform the action.* |  |
| **Ask:** | What will be the next step? |
| *Elicit from your learner that a 10-cluster must be formed from some of the balls in the top right quadrant and carried over to the top left quadrant. Note: your learner should* |  |

| | |
|---|---|
| just tell you, without yet performing the action. | |
| *Say:* | OK, so your next step is to get 10 balls to make the cluster. Here's a way of doing this. |
| *Direct your learner's attention to the line of ten. Have your learner place the clay rope between the two balls furthest from them – i.e. between the 9th and 10th ball.* | |
| *Point at the nine balls assembled in your learner's top right quadrant.* *Ask:* | If you have 9 balls here, how many more do you need to make up 10? |
| *If your learner hesitates, direct their attention to the* line of ten, *where the rope is now showing that 9 + 1 = 10. Discuss as needed.* | |
| *When your learner is certain that the answer is 1, if not immediately obvious to your learner,* *Ask:* | Where are you going to get the extra 1 ball from? |

| | |
|---|---|
| *Your learner should respond: from the 3 balls set apart from the 9 in the same quadrant.* | |
| *Once your learner has given the correct response,* **Say:** | OK – take 1 ball from here (*point to the 3 balls*), bring it to here (*point to the 9 balls*), then form a 10-cluster. |
| *When this has been done,* **Ask:** | In the order we have created here, what is the proper place for a 10-cluster? |
| *Your learner should indicate their top left quadrant.* | |
| *Once your learner has given the correct response,* **Say:** | OK – move the 10-cluster to its proper place. |
| *Once this is done, point to the 2 balls remaining in your learner's top right quadrant and* **Ask:** | How many are left here? |

| | |
|---|---|
| *Once your learner has answered,*     **Ask:** | What step remains to be done to complete the addition? |
| *Your learner should respond: move the three 10-clusters that are in their bottom left quadrant up to the top left quadrant.* | |
| *Once your learner has given the correct response,* <br><br>        **Say:** | OK – do that. |
| *When done, write an = sign after 29 + 33. Pass the paper and a pencil to your learner, and*    **Ask:** | Would you like to write the answer after the equal sign? |
| *When this is done, point to the 29 + 33 on the piece of paper.*     **Say:** | OK, now put the balls back as they were at the beginning, to show the problem 29 + 33. |
| *When this is done,*    **Ask:** | Do you feel ready to close your eyes and run a mental movie of what you did to solve this one? Whenever you need to, you can open your eyes and do the steps for real. |

| | |
|---|---|
| *If your learner says no, ask what would be needed for your learner to feel ready. Supply or assist with whatever is needed.* | |
| *Once your learner feels ready, have your learner run through their mental movie with eyes closed, peeking and moving the clay as needed. Have your learner describe each step from their mental movie.* | |
| *Continue in the same way with further addition examples that require carrying (exchanging). At any sign of hesitation or confusion, remind your learner to check tools, open their eyes and perform the addition in the clay.* | |
| *When your learner is confidently solving such equations using mental imagery, have your learner carefully move all balls, clusters and clay ropes to one side and move on to the exercise scripted in the next chapter.* | |

## Chapter 10: Adding In Reverse — Mental Subtraction

Once a person has mastered mental addition up to a total of 100, the next step is to master mental subtraction. If addition is 'leapfrog counting' forwards, subtraction is the same thing backwards. Subtracting 3 from 18 is the same as counting down from 18 to 15, but skipping 17 and 16.

Once again, the first step is to have a clear mental image of what subtracting is. A simple definition of subtract could be to take an amount from another amount. Just like adding, subtracting is a type of change and, therefore, consequence.

The following script, based on the Davis Maths Mastery Approach, is an example of how I help my clients to achieve fluency in mental subtraction. Once again, notice how the concepts of order and disorder are referenced:

| DO or OBSERVE: | SAY: |
|---|---|
| *As was done in the addition procedure above with the = and + symbols, follow the same procedure with the – symbol, including a real-world model and using the words subtract and minus.* | |
| *Have your learner re-create the cross shape out of rope that was used in the addition exercise, once again creating four quadrants on the table.*<br><br>***Say:*** | <br><br>In the last exercise, we agreed on an order. We are going to maintain a similar order in this next exercise. |
| *Establish that your learner can confidently identify the two quadrants on their left as proper places for 10-clusters, and the two quadrants on their right as the proper places for single balls. Assist with prompts as needed.* | |
| ***Say:*** | Now, when one amount is going to be subtracted from another, the proper place for the initial amount is here (*sweep* |

| | |
|---|---|
| | your hand over the two quadrants furthest from your learner). |
| **Say:** | When you subtract something from what is here (sweep your hand over the two quadrants furthest from your learner), the amount you subtract will go here (sweep your hand over the two quadrants closest to your learner). That will be the proper place for the amount you subtract. OK? |
| **Say:** | What is left here (sweep your hand over the two quadrants furthest from your learner) will be the answer. Any questions before we try this out for real? |
| On a piece of paper, write 23 – 12. Show this to your learner. **Say:** | Place 23 up at the top (sweep your hand over the two quadrants furthest from your learner). Do you remember the proper places for the 10-clusters and the single balls? |
| Provide guidance as needed. | |

| | |
|---|---|
| *Once the amount has been laid out in the proper order, point to the problem on the paper and* **Say:** | Now you can subtract the 12. Take the amount from here (*sweep your hand over the two quadrants furthest from your learner*), and move them to here (*sweep your hand over the two quadrants nearest to your learner*). |
| When this is done, **Say:** | The answer to the problem is what is left here (*sweep your hand over the two quadrants furthest from your learner*). |
| *In those two quadrants, there should now be one ten (top left for your learner) and one single ball (top right for your learner). Sweep your hand once again over the two quadrants furthest from your learner and* **Ask:** | How many? |
| *Elicit the answer: 11.* | |
| *On the piece of paper showing 23 – 12, write an = sign. Pass paper and pencil to your learner, and.* **Ask:** | Would you like to write |

| | |
|---|---|
| | the answer after the equal sign? |
| *Allow your learner to do so.* | |
| *On a piece of paper, write 11 + 12.* **Say:** | This is an addition problem that we did earlier. Will you show it to me again? |
| *Allow your learner to perform the addition. Your learner may well realise that this is a 'movie in reverse' of the subtraction sum just performed. If not, discuss until your learner comes to this realisation.* | |
| *On a piece of paper, write 54 – 21.* **Say:** | Now show me 54 – 21. |
| *At the start, your learner should place 5 ten-clusters in the quadrant to their top left, and 4 single balls in the quadrant to their top right.* *Have your learner perform the subtraction in the same way as in the earlier example. Your learner should move 2 ten-clusters from top left to bottom left, and 1 single ball from top right to bottom right.* | |

| | |
|---|---|
| Note: It does not matter whether your learner first moves the tens or first the units. This is not an exercise in the rules and sequence of written arithmetic; it is geared at developing spontaneous mental arithmetic ability through picture-thinking. | |
| *When done, write an = sign after 54 – 21. Pass the paper and a pencil to your learner and invite them to write down the answer.* | |
| *Continue in the same way with further subtraction problems until your learner is solving such problems fluently and confidently and recognises they are doing so. At this stage, avoid subtraction examples that require borrowing (exchanging).* | |
| *Once your learner is solving the examples fluently,* **Say:** | Just like you discovered earlier with the addition problems, when you don't have clay to hand and need to solve a subtraction of this kind, you can do so in just the same way, but using your |

|  | imagination. Are you ready to try? |
|---|---|
| *If your learner says 'No,' continue with further examples as practised above. Once your learner responds 'Yes,' proceed to the next step.* | |
| *On a piece of paper, re-write the last subtraction problem that was demonstrated by your learner in clay, **without the answer**. Have your learner set up the problem in clay, **without proceeding to the answer**.* | |
| *Say:* | Close your eyes and picture what you did in the clay to solve the problem. If you picture it clearly, talk me through your mental movie. If it doesn't come clearly, open your eyes and redo it in the clay for real, then tell me the answer. |
| *Once your learner has given you the correct answer with certainty, write an equal sign after the subtraction problem* | |

| | |
|---|---|
| *and invite the client to write the answer.* | |
| *Continue in the same way with further subtraction problems. At this stage, avoid subtraction problems that require borrowing (exchanging). When your learner is confidently solving subtraction problems using mental imagery, move on.* | |
| *On a piece of paper, write 31 - 18. Show this to your learner. Instruct your learner to lay out this problem in the quadrants.*      ***Say:*** | Show me this problem on the quadrants. How would you solve this one? |
| *As your learner starts to solve the problem on the grid, they should recognise a problem: there is only one single ball in the top right quadrant, whereas the subtraction problem requires eight single balls to be moved from top right to bottom right. Discuss this in as much detail as is needed.*      ***Say:*** | To solve this subtraction problem, we are going to need to create temporary |

| | |
|---|---|
| | disorder. We need this temporary disorder to move from one form of order to another. |
| *Instructing as needed, have your learner take a 10-cluster from their top left (tens) quadrant, separate it into single balls, and move it over to their top right (units) quadrant. There should now be 11 single balls in that quadrant. When done,* **Ask:** | Do you now have enough balls here (*point to your learner's top right quadrant*) to subtract the 8? |
| *Your learner should answer: 'Yes.' If the answer is 'No,' discuss and explore further as needed to facilitate clarity. Then* **Say:** | Go ahead and subtract the 8. |
| *When this has been done, instructing as needed, have your learner finish solving the problem by moving a 10-cluster from their top left quadrant down to their bottom left quadrant. When done, write an = sign after 31 – 18. Pass the* | |

| | | |
|---|---|---|
| *paper and a pencil to your learner.* | | |
| | *Ask:* | Would you like to write the answer after the equal sign? |
| *Continue in the same way with further subtraction examples that require borrowing (exchanging), until your learner is solving such examples fluently and confidently and recognises they are doing so.* | | |
| | *Say:* | Just as with the earlier problems you solved, you will be able to do this using your imagination if we put in one further piece. |
| | *Say:* | Just like earlier with addition, the problem with this type of subtraction is that there is a moment when you have to create temporary disorder in the place where you are collecting the units (*point to the quadrant that is top right for your learner*). When this happens, there can be as many as 18 balls in that place, and that can be |

| | |
|---|---|
| | difficult to picture. But just like with addition, by putting in an extra piece, we can make this easy. |
| *Return to the line of ten made earlier and*      **Ask:** | How many in this line? |
| *(Your learner should confidently answer, 'Ten,' because he created the line out of a 10-cluster and already used it for addition in the previous exercise.)* | |
| *On a piece of paper, write 62 – 33. Show this to your learner and*      **Say:** | Lay out 62 here (*sweep your hand over the two quadrants furthest from your learner*). |
| *Once the problem has been laid out,*      **Say:** | While you solve this one, let's talk it through step by step. What is the first step? |
| *Elicit from your learner that a 10-cluster from the top left quadrant is to be separated into single balls and moved into the top right quadrant.* | |
| **Say:** | OK, go ahead and move the 10 balls to here (*sweep your hand over the* |

111

| | |
|---|---|
| | quadrant that is top right for your learner), but this time, set them apart from the 2 balls that are already there. |
| *Allow your learner to perform the action.* | |
| ***Ask:*** | What will be the next step? |
| *Elicit from your learner that 3 balls will need to be moved from top right to bottom right.* Note: your learner should just tell you, without yet performing the action. | |
| ***Say:*** | OK, so your next step is to subtract 3 balls. Here's a way of doing this. |
| *Direct your learner's attention to the line of ten. Have your learner place the piece of clay rope between the 7th and 8th ball.* | |
| *Point at the 10 balls that are set apart in your learner's top right quadrant.* ***Ask:*** | If you have 10 balls here, how many will you have left after taking 3 out? |

| | |
|---|---|
| *If your learner hesitates, direct their attention to the* line of ten, *where the rope is now showing that 10 – 3 = 7. Discuss as needed.* | |
| *When your learner is certain that the answer is 7,* **Ask:** | So when there are 7 left here (*point at the 10 from which the 3 will be taken*) and 2 here (*point at the 2 balls that are set apart from the 10*), how many altogether will be left here (*sweep over the entire top right quadrant*)? |
| *If your learner responds with certainty: '9', move on. If your learner seems uncertain, explore the actions for real in the clay until your learner is certain.* | |
| *Once your learner has given the correct response with certainty,* **Say:** | OK – take 3 balls from here (*point to the 10 balls*) and subtract them to here (*point to the quadrant that is bottom right for your learner*). |

| | |
|---|---|
| *Once this is done, point to the 9 balls remaining in your learner's top right quadrant and* **Ask:** | How many are left here? |
| *Once your learner has answered,* **Ask:** | What step remains to be done to finish solving the problem? |
| *Your learner should respond: move 3 of the 10-clusters that are in their top left quadrant down to the bottom left quadrant.* | |
| *Once your learner has given the correct response,* **Say:** | OK – show me. |
| *When this has been done, the top two quadrants will show the answer: 29.* | |
| *Write an = sign after 62 – 33. Pass the paper and a pencil to your learner, and* **Ask:** | Would you like to write the answer after the equal sign? |
| *When this is done, point to the 62 – 33 on the piece of paper.* **Say:** | OK, now put the balls back as they were at the beginning, to show the problem 62 – 33. |

| | |
|---|---|
| *When this is done,* **Ask:** | Do you feel ready to close your eyes and run a mental movie of what you did to solve this one? Whenever you need to, you can open your eyes and do the steps for real. |
| *If your learner says no, ask what would be needed for your learner to feel ready. Supply or assist with whatever is needed.* | |
| *Once your learner feels ready, have your learner run through their mental movie with eyes closed, peeking and moving the clay as needed. Have your learner describe each step from their mental movie.* | |
| *Continue in the same way with further subtraction examples that require borrowing (exchanging). At any sign of hesitation or confusion, remind your learner to check tools, open their eyes and perform the addition in the clay.* | |

# Chapter 11: Onwards and Upwards — Multiplying and Dividing Mentally

Once mental addition and subtraction have been mastered, the next step is multiplication. In essence, multiplication is adding in groups. It is the process of starting at zero and adding the same number a certain number of times.

Once again, mental multiplication needs to be mastered before written multiplication can be. 'Long' multiplication on paper is simply a series of single-digit multiplications, each of which must be solved mentally and then recorded in the right place on the page.

The highest single-digit multiplication is 9 x 9, resulting in 81. Normally, however, children are taught to multiply mentally up to 10 x 10. Multiplying by 10 rarely poses problems: as our numeral system operates in base ten, even children with mathematical challenges tend to learn quickly that, when the multiplier is 10, one simply adds a 0 onto the end of the multiplicand to obtain the answer.

In some countries, the UK included, children are commonly trained in mental addition up to 12 x 12. Presumably, this dates back to the days of imperial measurements, in which twelve inches make a foot and twelve pence make a shilling. Nowadays, teaching times tables up to 12 is a rather arbitrary decision: multiplying by 11 and 12 can be solved in two steps on paper, in just the same way as multiplying by 13 or by any of the other two-digit multipliers which are not included in times table teaching.

In principle, all multiplication could be solved as repeated additions, recorded on paper. However, the ability to solve mentally up to 9 x 9 is useful. It cuts out a potentially enormous number of steps in long multiplication that would be necessary if our only mental skill was adding.

However, for those with mathematical challenges, times table are torture. Trying to learn multiplication facts when mathematical logic, counting, addition and subtraction skills are missing or incomplete is like taking a child who keeps falling off their bike and suggesting they have a go on a unicycle. I regularly see children torment themselves trying to remember the answer to a times table question that they never understood in the first place.

A physician's actions are governed by the Hippocratic axiom, primum non nocere ('First, do no harm.') But what about us educators? When I became a teacher, nobody asked me to sign an oath of non-maleficence. If educators were required to 'do no harm', then we would not be training children to memorise an answer before they had understood the question. Doing this is not education, but the opposite: an intellectual numbing. It is a message to children that 'doing well' is not about thinking critically, but rather about blind trust in your elders and betters. Mathematics is a thing of beauty to be explored and savoured; instead, the impatient rigidity of the school curriculum is making children swallow it like a bitter-tasting pill.

In the Davis approach, when helping a mathematically challenged learner to master multiplication facts, the first task is to create the conditions for the learner to see the answer to each times table problem — not as a set of numerals and symbols, but as a quantity. Working with the learner, we set up a grid of 10 x 10 clay balls. We make two clay ropes that can be laid across between rows and columns to 'trap' various quantities within the grid.

Using this tool, any multiplication fact up to 10 x 10 can be explored empirically. Lay one rope down after the third column and the other rope above the eighth row, and you're seeing 8 x 3. Not sure what the answer is? The quantity is in front of you, so you can quite simply count it.

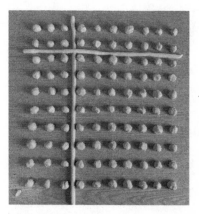

*Fig. 10 The Davis multiplication grid set to show the multiplication fact 8 x 3 = 24.*
*The little dab of clay in the bottom left corner is marking the place where this learner would start counting if they were to count all the balls in the grid.*

Not sure whether 8 x 3 is the same as 3 x 8? Just stand up, move 90 degrees round the table and look at it from the new angle: the rows have become columns, and the columns rows — so 8 x 3 has become 3 x 8 — but the quantity is still the same.

As a learner becomes ever more familiar and proficient with the Davis multiplication grid, I will often invite them to experiment with the addition and subtraction skills (acquired in the exercises scripted in the previous chapters). Where the answer to a multiplication problem is not immediately obvious, you may be able to get there by adding or subtracting from a nearby point of certainty.

For example, you may be uncertain of the answer to 8 x 3 but certain of the answer to 10 x 3. By briefly removing the rope partition above the 8th row...

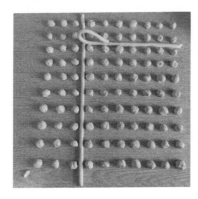

...you can now see 10 x 3, which you may well already be certain is 30.

Now replace the partition above the 8th row.

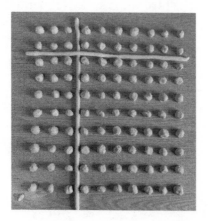

You are separating the 30 balls into two amounts. Above the row, you may easily recognise 6 balls. Below the row, therefore, you have 30 — 6 balls, which is 24.

As another option, if the learner is certain that 4 x 3 is 12, they might create an additional thinner rope partition above the 4th row.

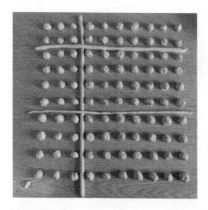

Now the quantity 8 x 3 has been separated into two sections containing 12 balls each. 12 + 12 is 24.

Now, frustrated maths teachers — I hear you — you have tried this approach with learners in the past, and it has failed. Doing this the Davis way, several things will be different this time:

1. The learner now has a set of mental tools that turn off disorientation. They can now bring mental distractions, perceptual distortion and 'mind fog' under control.
2. The learner has mastered the concepts of change, consequence, time, sequence and order and can now think with these concepts.
3. The learner has just been through a richly experiential process to acquire fluency and accuracy in counting, adding and subtracting — something that will previously have been lacking.
4. The learner has a grid in front of them showing the actual quantities involved in the multiplication they are solving.

As we saw earlier, a typical cognitive hallmark of mathematical learning difficulties is working memory restrictions. The Davis approach to mathematics essentially bypasses these restrictions: as the information required is physically on the table, in concrete form, it no longer has to be held and manipulated in the mind.

In place of the shaky foundations of mental manipulations and half-memorised facts, the following can now occur:

— A multiplication problem is laid out on the Davis multiplication grid;
— The problem is explored in the real world until the answer is discovered by the learner;
— The learner becomes ever more familiar with the process;
— With guidance as needed, the learner starts to discover that they have options for knowing each multiplication answer with certainty. They can count, or they can add or subtract from a nearby point of certainty.

In my experience, as this process progresses, the learner starts to remember ever more multiplication facts: not as memorised information, but as experiences that the learner themselves created. By created, I mean that the learner themselves devised their own route to knowing the answer with certainty, from a range of options available. It is quite common for the whole process to start to feel like a game.

Once a learner has mastered each multiplication fact with certainty, the Davis multiplication grid becomes a Davis division grid. For most mathematically challenged learners, up to this point division has been their greatest torment. Now, mastering division becomes a baby step that easily maps on top of the new certainty with multiplication that has been acquired. Take the multiplication problem 8 x 3 = 24 that was considered earlier:

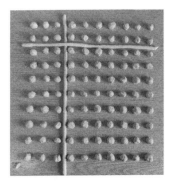

The same balls in the same layout can represent a division problem. It is simply a matter of starting with the total quantity of balls (24) and the number of balls in each row (3). This now represents the division problem 24 ÷ 3. What we are now trying to find out is: how many rows of 3 are contained in 24? That is simply the number of balls going up the side (8). So 24 ÷ 3 = 8. What is more, if we move 90 degrees round the table, so rows become columns, and columns rows, we can see that 24 ÷ 8 = 3.

Typically, it takes my learners around half an hour to master division of quantities up to 100. My humble message to curriculum planners: let the early stages take the time they need, and your patience will be rewarded.

## Chapter 12: The Little Stuff — Fractions and Decimals

One of the powerful things about plasticine clay as a manipulative is that you can cut it into ever smaller pieces. This is immensely helpful for exploring quantities less than 1.

In all the Davis Maths Mastery exercises up to this point, 1 has been represented by a clay ball. Now, a clay ball can be squashed into a disk. Using a clay cutter, the learner can cut the disk into halves. Then they can cut the halves in half to make quarters. They can continue cutting in half to make eighths, and then sixteenths. Finally, they can re-roll the clay into a disk and see if they can figure out how to cut it into three equal pieces, to make thirds.

For some older learners, it can be useful to explore the concepts of numerator and denominator and to examine the very different functions of the numerals above and below the fraction line. Reaching clarity on this now will equip a learner to better understand what is happening when they learn the techniques for adding, subtracting, multiplying and dividing fractions on paper.

Below is an example of how I sometimes go about this process with a learner. Included also is an example of how the clay can be used to explore how to add unequal fractions by identifying a common denominator.

| DO or OBSERVE: | SAY: |
|---|---|
| *Say* <br><br> *Do the same thing yourself, but cut your disc unevenly into two.* | Make a clay disc and cut it in half. |
| *Ask* | is mine also half? |
| *The answer should be:* no, as the pieces are unequal in size. | |
| *Say* | In maths, all quantities are measured in relation to the idea of *one*. 2 means *one and another one*. 3 means *one and another one and another one*. It is easy to measure numbers bigger than 1 using this standard, but what happens when we try to measure quantities less than one? <br><br> If you want to measure an amount less than one, |

| | |
|---|---|
| | you can`t measure it in 1s as it is less than 1. The only way you can measure pieces less than 1 is by knowing how many of those pieces you need to make one. |
| *On a piece of paper, write ½ as fraction and show which is the **numerator** (1) and **denominator** (2).* | |
| ***Say*** | The **denominator** tells you how many of these pieces you would need to make 1. In other words, it tells you the *size* of the piece in relation to one. |
| ***Say*** | The **numerator** shows you how many of these pieces we have. |
| *Have the client cut the disc in 4 and then remove 3 of the resulting quarters.* | |
| ***Ask*** | How many pieces are left? (*1*) How many such pieces would we need to make a whole 1? (*4*) We would call this fraction 'one quarter' and we would write it as ¼ (*show* |

| | | |
|---|---|---|
| | | *this to the client on paper).* |
| | *Say* | So we now know that the size of what we are measuring is one quarter the size of 1 (1 being the whole we started with), so we know how many pieces we have as well as the size of the pieces.<br><br>Fractions are a way of measuring a quantity less than one. |
| *To reinforce the idea of measuring/comparing numbers less than one, have the client make three equal discs. (You can help as appropriate).* | | |
| | *Say* | These three discs represent 3. One, and another one, and another one. |
| *Isolate one of the two discs and cut it in half. Isolate one of the halves and* | *Say* | Here, we have something twice smaller than 1. We would need two of these to make 1. This is ½. |

| | | |
|---|---|---|
| | *Say* | Take one of the other discs and cut it in half, then to quarters. Can you now cut it to eighths? (*Give guidance as appropriate.*) |
| *Write 1/2 and 1/8 on paper.* | *Ask* | Does it make sense that, the bigger the number on the bottom, the smaller the pieces are? So if I had one millionth (*write 1/1,000,000 on paper*), would that be a big piece or a small piece? (*small*) |
| *Discard the disc cut into eighths, but keep the disc cut into halves.* *Take the third disc and cut into thirds. Place it near to the disc cut into halves.* | *Say* | Suppose we wanted to add one of these (*isolate and point to one of the thirds*) to one of these (*isolate and point to one of the halves*). To add fractions together, they have to have a common denominator. You can`t add 1/3 + 1/2, because they are |

| | |
|---|---|
| | different sized pieces which don't fit into one another. |
| | You have to add like with like. |
| *Say* | Cut each of the thirds in half. |
| *Have your learner do this.* | |
| *Ask* | How many of these pieces would you need to make 1? (*Answer : 6*). |
| *Ask* | Can you work out how we would write this fraction? (*1/6*) Do you know what it is called? *(You are looking for the answer: 'one sixth' or 'sixths').* |
| *Ensure the 6 sixths are still together, arranged 'pizza slice style', so the original disc can still be seen.*<br><br><br><br>*Ask* | If you want to, can you still pull out thirds from this disc? |

| | | |
|---|---|---|
| *If the client is uncertain, demonstrate how 2 sixths are still the same* amount *as 1 third.* | | |
| | ***Say*** | When adding fractions together, you can add together the numerators (the number of parts you have out of the whole amount), but only if the denominator is the same for both fractions.<br><br>So to add one half you will have to change the fractions to make the denominator the same. |
| *Return to the disc cut into halves. Cut each half into thirds.* ***Ask*** | | How many of these pieces would you need to make 1? (*Answer : 6*). Can you work out how we would write this fraction ? (*1/6*) What is it called ? (« *one sixth* » or « *sixths* »).<br><br>So now, the two discs are cut into the same piece size – right ? |

| | |
|---|---|
| *Ensure the six sixths are still together, arranged so the original disc can be seen.* | |
| **Ask** | If you want to, can you still pull out halves from this? *(If your learner is uncertain, demonstrate how three sixths are still the same* amount *as one half.)* |
| **Ask** | Can you now add together one half and one third? *(As appropriate, guide your learner to take three sixths from one disc and two sixths from the other.)* Can you see the answer? (5/6). |
| **Say** | What we just did was to find what is called a *common denominator* between one half and one third. Remember, the *denominator* is the bottom number in the fraction, which shows us the piece size. A *common denominator* is a size of piece that fits into either |

| | |
|---|---|
| | of the fractions we have to add together.<br><br>What was the *common denominator* we found for this sum? |
| *When your learner has answered correctly, write 6 below a fraction line on a piece of paper:*<br><br><br><br>**Ask**<br><br>*If your learner is uncertain, demonstrate how none of the lower numbers (/5, /4 etc.) would work for adding halves and thirds.* | Is 6 the lowest number we could use here (point to the /6 on the paper) to solve this sum? |
| **Say** | That means that sixths were the *lowest common denominator* we could use to solve this sum. There is no lower number that would work here as the denominator – right? If your maths teacher uses the words '*lowest common denominator*', will you |

| | know what [he/she] means now? |
|---|---|
| *As appropriate, explore some other simple sums for adding fractions by finding the lowest common denominator. If appropriate, you could practise subtracting fractions using the same technique.* | |

Plasticine clay is equally powerful as a medium for mastering decimal fractions. In Chapter 8, we looked at how a learner can use the clay to create units, tens and hundreds as quantities, together with the numerals that represent them, in order to become fluent and agile at operating with base ten place value.

From a unit — a single ball — it is equally possible to go in the other direction. A learner can take a plasticine ball...

...roll it into a 'rope'...

...then cut the rope into ten equal pieces.

One of those pieces represents one tenth, or 0.1.

One of the tenths can then be rolled into a smaller 'string'...

...and similarly cut into ten equal pieces.

One of these pieces represents one hundredth, or 0.01.

With a bit of manual dexterity and patience, it is even possible to cut a hundredth piece into ten, to make thousandths.

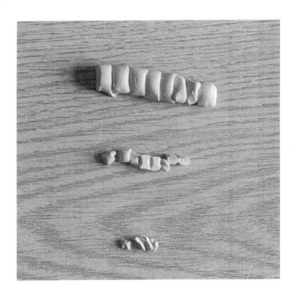

Along with the quantities one hundred, one ten and one one laid out earlier, one tenth and one hundredth can now be laid out in their proper places, with a decimal point and numerals added, to create a rich visual experience of the actual quantities that decimals represent.

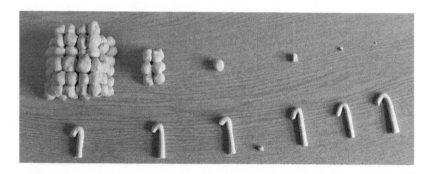

This process is a routine part of a Davis Maths Mastery Programme. I have seen countless learners reach a new clarity around the meaning of decimals and how to work with them. After this, transitioning to adding, subtracting, multiplying and dividing quantities that include decimal fractions is usually quite effortless. That is what happens when a learner is not just told mathematical facts and conventions, but is allowed to recreate them for themselves.

# Chapter 13: The Literacy of Numeracy — Maths In Reading And Writing

Many years ago, I remember conducting a Davis Dyslexia Programme with a boy who had struggled with both literacy and numeracy. While the boy and his family were keen to use the Davis approach to improve his reading and writing, he had undertaken another programme, using a different approach, which had radically improved his paper-based arithmetic.

While with me, the boy demonstrated the results of this programme, which were impressive. At lightning speed, he was able to tackle three-digit multiplication sums, producing a correct answer quicker than I could.

However, his family told me that he still struggled with word-based mathematical problems. They were unsure whether the root cause pointed to difficulties with reading or difficulties with maths. Therefore, once the Davis approach had significantly improved his reading, we took a look, using some text book maths story problems. I remember to this day the first problem that we looked at:

Jake earns £100. Joe earns £20 less than Jake. How much does Joe earn?

The boy was stumped. He simply could not 'see' that this was a straightforward subtraction problem. If he had realised this, he would have been able to solve it in a matter of seconds.

For many mathematically challenged learners, maths story problems pose the biggest problem of all. Here, it is not enough to be able to do arithmetic. To solve a maths story problem, you need to:

— Read the problem scenario
— Picture the problem scenario (precisely, in every detail)
— Work out what arithmetic is required to solve the problem
— Do the arithmetic.

**Picture-At-Punctuation** is a simple Davis technique which enhances both comprehension and retention of what we read. A person's perceptual ability can be used as a talent in this technique. The principles behind the technique are straightforward:

— Punctuation marks indicate the end of a complete thought;
— A complete thought can be either pictured or felt. The words: 'There was a woman standing by the...' do not

evoke a complete mental image. The complete sentence: 'There was a woman standing by the kiosk.' does;

— Punctuation marks provide the opportunity to stop and check if a detailed, accurate in meaning mental image (picture or feeling) has been consciously made and understood;

— To comprehend words or text, we have to know what they represent; consciously or unconsciously, we must convert the words that we read or hear into mental imagery.

Because of its precision, and the way in which it utilises a dyscalculic's natural picture-thinking strengths, Picture-At-Punctuation is a powerful tool for comprehending mathematical story problems. First, let us look at the general procedure as it applies to reading non-mathematical text, fictional or factual.

## PROCEDURE

1. Check your learner can recognise and knows to stop at the following punctuation marks:

   - Full stops
   - Exclamation marks
   - Question marks
   - Commas
   - Colons
   - Semicolons
   - Dashes

2. Give these instructions:

> We are going to explore how we understand what we read. To us, punctuation means 'picture the meaning'. When you see a punctuation mark, stop and make a picture in your mind of what you have just read.

- o Have your learner read up to the first punctuation mark.
- o Stop your learner from looking at the words just read. (Cover the words with your hand if you need to do so.)
- o Ask your learner, *What do you see?*
- o If the words just read make something that is not easily pictured – such as *Long ago*, or *Once upon a time*, ask: *What do you feel?* or *What does that mean to you?*

3. Check that the description your learner gives is accurate and precise. No extra, irrelevant information should be in the picture. It should reflect just what the writer intended the reader to have.

4. Repeat the procedure until all the sentences in the paragraph have been pictured.

Normally, a person wishing to comprehend mathematical story problems will first need to practise Picture-At-Punctuation on one or more non-mathematical texts that are easy to picture. Literary texts rich in imagery are often a good place to start. For teenagers and adults, one of my personal favourites is the opening of Metamorphosis by Franz Kafka:

> One morning, when Gregor Samsa woke from troubled dreams, he found himself transformed in his bed into a horrible vermin. He lay on his armour-like back, and if he lifted his head a little he could see his brown belly, slightly domed and divided by arches into stiff sections. The bedding was hardly able to cover it and seemed ready to slide off any moment. His many legs, pitifully thin compared with the size of the rest of him, waved about helplessly as he looked.[30]

Stopping to make a mental picture at each comma and full stop here gives a vivid set of images around the bizarre transformation of this unfortunate individual and of the bed he is lying on.

Once a person is sufficiently familiar with the Picture-At-Punctuation technique, they can start to try it out on mathematical story problems. Here, however, there is one important difference. In a mathematical story problem we are trying, not just to comprehend the scenario, but in doing so, to 'see' what arithmetic we are going to need. To do this, we do not just need a crystal-clear picture of every detail in the text of the story problem; we need to carry on picturing all the details at once. It is by seeing how all the

---

[30] https://www.gutenberg.org/files/5200/5200-h/5200-h.htm

details are connected that we will work out what arithmetic is required.

Therefore, at the outset at least, I frequently recommend my learners to take a piece of paper and sketch out their pictures as they make them. Take this problem, for example:

> Paco took off in his helicopter from 400 metres above sea level. He later landed at a location 500 metres above sea level. What was Paco's change in altitude?

It may be that a learner can picture this without sketching it out. Or it may be that drawing a sketch along these lines would be helpful:

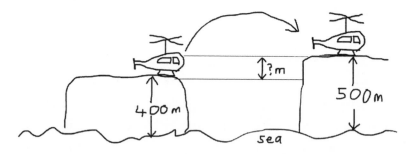

Sketching it out fixes all the details of your mental picture in one place and enables you to see what is involved: a subtraction to find the difference between 500m and 400m.

Now take this one:

Rachel is posting 18 flyers for the science club and 8 for the music club. She wants to make all the locations identical, with the same combination of science club flyers and music club flyers. In addition, she wants to make sure that no flyers are left over. What is the greatest number of locations that Rachel can post at?

There are several elements that can make this problem trickier than the last one. First, there are multiple moving pieces: flyers being posted in different locations. Secondly, there are two conditions: 'make all the locations identical' and 'no flyers left over'.

Thirdly, there are words that can be difficult to picture accurately. What does 'identical' mean here? Paint all the walls the same colour? No: we are told it means 'same combination'. But how obvious is the intended meaning of *combination*? Dictionary.com gives eight different definitions for the word. One of them, flagged as its mathematical meaning, is *the arrangement of elements into various groups without regard to their order in the group*. That seems to fit here. But how likely is a mathematically challenged individual to picture the one mathematical meaning of the word and not one of the other seven? Just to make matters worse, the phrase 'In addition', used here at the start of the third sentence, has a mathematical definition among others. But the intended meaning here is not the mathematical one.

Fourthly, the question is very context dependent. If you are a pupil at a school that has clubs, you may recognise what is going on. If you are lucky, you will realise that 'posting' means *putting up* or *leaving on display* and not *posting in a letter box*. If you are unlucky, you won't.

Fifthly, and possibly most significantly, there are *trigger words* in this passage that make crucial distinctions in meaning. In the Davis approach, a trigger word is a small, abstract word such as *as*, *for*, *with*, *the*, *if* etc. They are especially problematic for picture-thinking dyslexics and dyscalculics because they do not evoke a mental image for their meaning. Can you picture the meaning of *elephant*? Good. Now try picturing the meaning of *the*. Trickier, right? My first book, *Why* Tyrannosaurus *But Not* If*?* is named after the difficulties with these words and explores the issues involved in depth.

Let us look at the first sentence of the above problem again.

'Rachel is posting 18 flyers for the science club and 8 for the music club.'

Suppose you misread *for* as *at*? It immediately changes your picture for what is going on here. The resulting mis-picturing will torpedo your entire understanding of the remaining text.

For a mathematically challenged individual who is also dyslexic, there is a further problem. Every mental picture comes with a feeling attached. The blank picture accompanying each trigger word comes with a feeling of confusion. Half or more of the words in a typical English text are trigger words. Out of the 60 words of this particular problem question, 30 are trigger words. Typically, after a dyslexic reader's perception has been assaulted by several trigger words in rapid succession, the accumulated confusion disorientates them. The person is now reading in a state where their perception is distorted and their mental acuity compromised.

Story problems of this kind need to be addressed from multiple angles. First, it may be necessary, not just to sketch the problem, but to make it in the real world. Could your learner cut out 26 small rectangles out of paper and label 18 of them SC for 'science club' and the other 8 'MC' for 'music club'? This will enable your learner to 'become' Rachel and actually 'post' the 'flyers'. They may then discover that they can only create identical combinations at a maximum of 2 locations.

Note that making the problem in the real world and/or sketching it on paper is an interim step. Its purpose is not to turn every maths class into an arts and crafts session, but rather to help the learner habituate a pictorial way of thinking about these problems. Sooner or later, the learner will be able to picture most or all such problems mentally.

However, there is another piece to the puzzle. Your learner is going to need to fill in the blank pictures that accompany the small, abstract words in the maths problem. In a Davis Programme, we use a clay modelling technique known as Davis Symbol Mastery. For full instructions in the technique, see *The Gift of Learning* or

*The Gift of Dyslexia* by Ronald Davis or purchase a Davis Symbol Mastery Kit from your regional Davis office.

If your learner is 'just' dyscalculic, they are going to need to use Davis Symbol Mastery to model and master 25 words in their specifically mathematical meanings:

| | |
|---|---|
| a | between |
| about | by |
| and | each |
| as | even |
| be | for |
|   o  is | from |
|   o  are | into |
|   o  were | just |
|   o  will | less |
|   o  would | left |

This process enables a dyscalculic learner to understand these words in their mathematical meanings when they are used in story problems. For example, the word *a* can mean *one*; *one kind of*; *any one*; or it can have the very mathematical meaning, *for each*. In the sentence, 'Apples cost £2.50 a kilo', only the meaning *for each* makes sense. The word *by* has several meanings: one of these is *beside, next to*; but it also has the mathematical meaning, *used as a multiplier of*. In the question, *What is three **by** two?*, a picture-thinker who went for the first meaning might well answer, 'Five', whereas the answer sought after is *six*. Just to make things worse, *by* can also mean, *into groups of*, which essentially means *used as a **divisor** of* — as in the instruction, *'Divide six **by** two'* — pretty much the opposite of its other mathematical meaning.

*Fig. 11: A model for the maths trigger word each, using the definition, 'every one of two or more people or things, thought of separately'. The example used here: each person has packed two boxes. The long rope loop emerging from the back of the head of the figure on the left represents a thought; the vertical lines show that each person and their packing is being thought of separately.*

If your learner is both dyscalculic and dyslexic, they will benefit from mastering the full list of 219 dyslexia trigger words listed by Ronald Davis in his book, *The Gift of Dyslexia*. People with reading challenges frequently slip up on these words, and this can affect their answers in mathematics too. Nina Pitoska, a fellow Davis Facilitator who had previously been a mathematics teacher, cites a case where her class took a test that included the question, 'What is 25% of 32?' One dyslexic pupil replied: '24'. He had mistaken the word *of* for *off* – both of these words feature in the Davis trigger word list for dyslexia.

Helping a mathematically challenged learner to develop an effective approach to these story problems can be a gradual process. When the learner is also dyslexic, there is a further layer to the problem — reading — that also needs to be addressed. As a helper, understanding the factors that are currently making this process difficult for your learner is the first step. Once they are understood, they can be dealt with, one by one.

# Chapter 14: Beyond Arithmetic — Getting Creative with Other Branches of Mathematics

Arithmetic can be seen as the cornerstone of mathematics. Fluency and accuracy in arithmetic goes hand in hand with well-developed mathematical thinking and reasoning. A solid grasp of arithmetic is a prerequisite for understanding and mastering mathematics in general.

Nonetheless, there are many other branches of mathematics that need to be understood and mastered on a person's mathematical journey. In the UK, Key Stage 3 pupils (children aged 11 — 14) are taught topics encompassing: algebra; ratio, proportion, and rates of change; geometry and measures; probability; and statistics[31].

While mastering arithmetic will certainly make these topic areas more accessible, some learners will need further help to convert the principles of each topic area into mental imagery. This new gallery of mental imagery, combined with the person's new-found arithmetical skill,

---

[31] https://www.gov.uk/government/publications/national-curriculum-in-england-mathematics-programmes-of-study/national-curriculum-in-england-mathematics-programmes-of-study#year-3-programme-of-study

will then enable learners to solve individual problems in the given topic area.

## Algebra: Switching on the Pictures

Take algebra, for instance. One of the key principles of all mathematics is that the = sign means *equal* — that what is on one side of the sign is the same in amount as what is on the other side. Similarly, if you make the same change to what is on both sides of the sign, the amounts on each side will still be equal. It is true that 3 + 3 = 6. It is also true that 3 + 2 = 5. In the second statement, there is one less on each side of the equal sign compared with the first statement.

This principle — make the same change either side of the equal sign and it's still true — is the basis of much of the problem-solving we undertake in algebra. If you have a statement such as:

$x + 2 = 6$

...and you want to find the value of $x$, you want to 'unclutter' the left-hand side of the equation to get rid of everything there that isn't $x$. How? Subtract 2. But if you just subtract 2 from what is on the left, you are now telling mathematical porkies. You also need to subtract 2 from what is on the right. That gives you:

$= 4$

That sort of explanation might work for a word-thinking individual. For those picture thinkers who have lived for years with mathematical challenges, it probably will not. What will work is a set of concrete experiences that the learner themselves has created. What will work is clay.

Start by interviewing your learner. First, establish that your learner has come across algebra at school and knows what it is. Then, you might ask questions like these:

'Do you find algebra hard?'

If the answer is 'yes', ask:

'Would you like algebra to become easy? Would you like to learn how to *picture* what is going on in algebra, so you can solve algebra equations and know you've got the right answer?'

If the answer is yes, say:

'I think I can help you with this. Would you like me to try?'

As a starting point, you could have your learner make a *concrete metaphor* for the equal sign. A set of old-fashioned balance scales works particularly well.

Next, have your learner make an equal sign and place it in front of the scales or other object that was created.

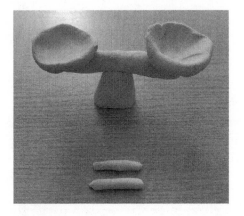

The next step is to agree on something that will represent the idea of 1. This could be a simple small disc, similar to the solid metal weights used on balance scales.

Have your learner make the numeral 1 and place it in front of the disc that they made. Have the learner point to the disc and say, 'You represent 1.'

Now have your learner make a supply of several more discs, so there are 6 — 8 in total.

### *Solving an Algebra Equation by Subtracting*

Have your learner place one of the discs on each side of the balance scale and lay out the symbols 1 = 1 in front. Have the learner point to the scales and say, 'You represent 1 = 1.'

Have your learner make a small everyday item that is easy to fashion out of clay. Here, a carrot has been chosen.

Have your learner make the first letter of the word and place it in front of the clayed item.

Have your learner point to the letter and say, 'You are [letter] meaning [word].' (Here: 'You are *c* meaning *carrot*.')

Have your learner place the carrot and two *1*s on the left scale pan, and four *1*s on the right scale pan.

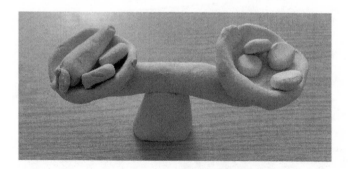

Discuss with your learner that the carrot is an *unknown weight*, which in mathematics is the same as an *unknown amount*. Explain that the job now is to find out the weight of the carrot.

Discuss with your learner that, on the left scale pan there is a carrot and two *1*s, and on the right scale pan there are four *1*s. Discuss with your learner that, mathematically, we could represent this as *c + 2 = 4*. Have your learner make this equation and place it in front of the scales.

Have your learner point to the scales and say, 'You represent *c + 2 = 4*.'

You are now going to discuss with your learner how to simplify the equation so that only *c* is on the left. Sometimes, I say something like this:

'Our job now is to change what's on the scales so that, on the left, there is only the carrot. At the moment, those two *1s* are getting in the way of seeing how much the carrot weighs, so they need to be removed.

'But imagine someone has planted a stink bomb in the fulcrum of the scales. If they go out of balance, they'll break the stink bomb and the kitchen will smell revolting for the next three days.'

'So if you're going to remove the two *1* 's from this side [point to the left scale pan], what do you need to do on this side to make sure the scales stay in balance?'

Most learners recognise immediately and intuitively that, if they take two *1* 's away from both sides, the scales will stay in balance. Once this is done, the value of *c* (the weight of the carrot) can be seen:

Your learner can now make *c = 2* out of clay and place it in front of the model:

Say to your learner, 'You took two *1* 's off each side. Mathematically, we can say you subtracted the same amount from each side — right? When you subtract the same amount from both sides of an equation, the two sides are still equal. If it's true that *c + 2 = 4*, it's also true that *c = 2.*'

### *Solving an Algebra Equation by Dividing*

Have your learner make two examples of another small everyday item. Here, two apples have been chosen.

Have your learner make the first letter of the word and place it in front of one of the two clayed items.

Have your learner point to the letter and say, 'You are [letter] meaning [word].' (Here: 'You are *a* meaning *apple*.'

Have your learner place the two apples on the left scale pan, and six *1*'s on the right scale pan.

Discuss with your learner that, on the left scale pan there are two apples, and on the right scale pan there are six *1*'s. Discuss with your learner that, mathematically, we could represent this as *2a = 6*. Have your learner make this equation and place it in front of the scales.

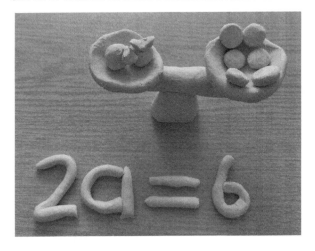

Have your learner point to the scales and say, 'You represent *2a = 6*.'

Say to your learner:

'Our job now is to change what's on the scales so that, on the left, there is only one apple. Then we will be able to see what one apple weighs.

'But remember — when we make a change to the scales, if they go out of balance, they'll break the stink bomb and the kitchen will smell revolting for the next three days.

'So if you're going to change this side [*point to the left scale pan*] from two apples down to one apple, what do you need to do on this side to make sure the scales stay in balance?'

Some learners recognise immediately and intuitively that, if they take away *half* the contents of each scale pan, the scales will stay in balance. Others may try to remove one apple from the left and one *1* from the right. If this occurs, stop the learner and say:

'Careful — you're removing different things from each side. One of these [point to the apples] may not weigh the same as one of these [point to the *1* 's]. What can you do instead — what change can you make to both sides that keeps the scales in balance?'

Once your learner has figured out what to do, the value of *a* (the weight of the apple) can be seen:

Your learner can now make *a = 3* out of clay and place it in front of the model:

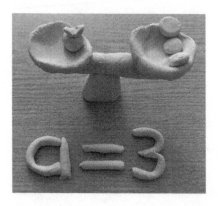

Say to your learner, 'You took *half* the contents off of each side. In other words, you *halved* what you had on each side. Mathematically, we can say you *divided* each side by the same number — by 2 — right? When you divide both sides of an equation by the same number, the two sides are still equal. If it's true that 2a = 6, it's also true that a = 3.'

### *Solving an Algebra Equation by Multiplying*

Have your learner make an everyday item that could be cut in half. Here, a loaf of bread has been chosen.

Have your learner make the first letter of the word and place it in front of the clayed item.

Have your learner point to the letter and say, 'You are [letter] meaning [word].' (Here: 'You are *b* meaning a loaf of *bread*.'

Have your learner cut the item in half.

Explain to your learner that half of b is written as $\frac{b}{2}$ . As necessary, write this on a piece of paper and show it to your learner. Then have your learner make the symbols out of clay and place them in front of the half-loaf.

Have your learner place one half of the loaf on the left scale pan, and two *1*'s on the right scale pan.

Discuss with your learner that, on the left scale pan there is half a loaf of bread, and on the right scale pan there are two *1* 's. Discuss with your learner that, mathematically, we could represent this as $\frac{b}{2} = 2$. Have your learner make this equation and place it in front of the scales.

Have your learner point to the scales and say, 'You represent $\frac{b}{2} = 2$.'

Say to your learner:

'Our job now is to change what's on the scales so that, on the left, there is a whole loaf. Then we will be able to see what one loaf of bread weighs.

'But remember about the stink bomb. So if you're going to change this side [point to the left scale pan] from half a loaf to a whole loaf, what do you need to do on this side to make sure the scales stay in balance?'

Typically, learners recognise immediately and intuitively that, if they *double* the contents of each scale pan, the scales will stay in balance.

Once your learner has figured out what to do, the value of b (the weight of one whole loaf of bread) can be seen:

Your learner can now make *b = 4* out of clay and place it in front of the model:

Say to your learner, 'You *doubled* the contents on each side. Mathematically, we can say you *multiplied* each side by the same number — by 2 — right? When you multiply both sides of an equation by the same number, the two sides are still equal. If it's true that $\frac{b}{2}$ = 2, it's also true that b = 4.'

### *Solving an Algebra Equation by Adding*

Have your learner make an everyday item that a piece or slice could be cut out of. Here, a cake has been chosen.

Have your learner make the first letter of the word and place it in front of the clayed item.

Have your learner point to the letter and say, 'You are [letter] meaning [word].' (Here: 'You are *c* meaning a *cake.*')

Have your learner cut a slice out of the cake.

Say to your learner, 'Let's imagine you weigh the cut-out slice and discover it weighs the same as *1.*' Have your learner place the cut-out slice onto the left-hand scale pan, and a *1* on the right-hand scale pan.

Have your learner place the symbols *1 = 1* in front of the scales.

Have your learner point to the slice and to the *1* and say, 'You are both equal. You are both *1*.'

Have your learner remove the slice and the *1* from the scales and put them to one side without destroying them. Have your learner remove the symbols *1 = 1*.

Direct your learner's attention back to the cake with the missing slice. Say to your learner, 'This used to be a whole cake, which you labelled as *c*, but now there is a slice cut out of it. That slice weighs *1*, right? So what is left is *c – 1*.'

Have your learner create *c – 1* out of clay and place it in front of the cake with the missing slice.

Have your learner place the cake with the missing slice on the left-hand scale pan and three *1* 's on the right-hand scale pan.

Discuss with your learner that, on the left scale pan there is a cake with a slice missing, and the slice weighs the same as *1*. Discuss that on the right scale pan there are three *1* 's. Discuss with your learner that, mathematically, we could represent this as *c − 1 = 3*. Have your learner make this equation and place it in front of the scales.

Have your learner point to the scales and say, 'You represent *c − 1 = 3*.'

Say to your learner:

'Our job now is to change what's on the scales so that, on the left, there is a whole cake. Then we will be able to see what one whole cake weighs.

'But remember about the stink bomb. So if you want to change this side [point to the left scale pan] so there is a whole cake there, what do you need to do to make sure the scales stay in balance?'

As needed, and without over-prompting, guide your learner to the recognition that, if they *add* the slice back into the cake on the left-hand scale pan, while also *adding* another 1 to the right-hand scale pan, the scales will stay in balance.

Once your learner has figured out what to do, the value of *c* (the weight of the whole cake) can be seen:

Your learner can now make *c* = 4 out of clay and place it in front of the model:

Say to your learner, 'Onto each scale pan, you placed something weighing 1. Mathematically, we can say you *added* the same amount to each side — right? When you add the same amount to both sides of an equation, the two sides are still equal. If it's true that $c - 1 = 3$, it's also true that $c = 4$.'

### Combining The Knowledge Gained

Your learner is now ready to experience solving algebra equations that involve two of the above operations in succession.

Have your learner make two examples of a small everyday item that is easy to fashion out of clay. Here, two sausages have been chosen.

Have your learner make the first letter of the word and place it in front of one of the two clayed items.

Have your learner point to the letter and say, 'You are [letter] meaning [word].' (Here: 'You are *s* meaning *sausage.*')

Have your learner place the two sausages and a *1* on the left scale pan, and five *1*'s on the right scale pan.

Discuss with your learner that, on the left scale pan there are two sausages and a *1*, and on the right scale pan there are five *1*'s. Discuss with your learner that, mathematically, we could represent this as *2s + 1 = 5*. Have your learner make this equation and place it in front of the scales.

Have your learner point to the scales and say, 'You represent *2s + 1 = 5.*'

Say to your learner:

'Our job now is to change what's on the scales so that, on the left, there is only one sausage. Then we will be able to see what one sausage weighs.

'But remember about the stink bomb. So when changing what is on the scales, always make sure they stay in balance.

'This time, you are going to have to make two changes, one after another. Can you see which change is easiest to make first?'

Some learners recognise immediately and intuitively that the easiest change is to remove a *1* from each side. Others may need some gentle guidance.

Once your learner has figured out what to do and removed a *1* from each side, there will be two sausages on the left and four *1* 's on the right.

From here, your learner may be able to proceed without prompting. If not, say something like this:

'Just like with the apples earlier, what remains to be done is to change what's on the scales so that, on the left, there is only one sausage. Then we will be able to see what one sausage weighs.

'Can you see what you need to do? Remember to keep the scales in balance.'

Once your learner has figured out what to do (i.e. halve the contents on each side), the value of $s$ (the weight of the sausage) can be seen:

Your learner can now make $s = 2$ out of clay and place it in front of the model:

Say to your learner, 'You successfully solved this equation in two steps.' Talk through what was done.

### *Moving Across to Paper*

Say to your learner, 'There is one further step we need to accomplish before you can start solving algebra equations on paper.

'When using the scales, you were making real objects — such as carrots, apples and sausages — and using a letter to represent each of them.

'At the beginning, we didn't know how much the objects weighed. Mathematically, that is like saying we have an *unknown amount* in the equation. Because it's an unknown amount, we can't represent it with a number. That's why it is represented with a letter.

'In the clay, we made real objects. But actually, when solving an equation, it doesn't matter what the object is. In the last one we did in clay, if you had used, say, strawberries instead of sausages, we would have gone through the exact same steps and got the same answer in the same way, right?'

'So when you are solving this type of equation on paper, the letter doesn't represent a particular real thing. We might think of it as representing *any* real thing. In algebra equations on paper, most often the letter used is $x$.

'Do you have any questions about what we are about to do?'

If your learner has any questions, answer them. Then ask:

'Do you feel ready to try some algebra on paper?'

If *no*, discuss what would be needed for your learner to feel ready, and supply what is needed. If *yes*, pass your learner some paper and some simple algebra equations such as the following ones:

| | |
|---|---|
| a) | $3x + 5 = 17$ |
| b) | $2x - 8 = 10$ |
| c) | $4x + 7 = 31$ |
| d) | $6x - 3 = 15$ |

Allow your learner to solve the equations. Be alert for signs of confusion or frustration. If confusion occurs, revert to the clay and assist your learner to certainty.

Of course, there are many further layers of complexity that your learner will encounter if they progress further with algebra. However, they will be equipped with a gallery of mental images that give clarity as to the function of each element in the equation and what steps to take in order to solve it.

## Ratios in Clay

A ratio is the number of times one thing occurs or exists compared with the number of times another thing occurs or exists. For example, when cooking, you might mix flour and water in a weight ratio of 2:1, meaning that you put twice as much flour by weight as you do water.

Just as with algebra, a purely word-based explanation such as the above may be insufficient for a picture-thinker. They may need to draw, or better still make, a real-world example. After that, they will be equipped with the necessary mental imagery to make sense of ratio problems as they encounter them in the classroom or elsewhere in life.

Let us start with a specific example. Here is one generated by AI for an 11-year-old:

'Ella is planning a pizza party for her friends. She wants to make sure there's enough pizza for everyone to enjoy. She decides to order two types of pizzas: cheese pizza and pepperoni pizza.

'Ella knows that her friends really love pepperoni, so she wants the ratio of pepperoni pizzas to cheese pizzas to be 3:2. This means for every 3 pepperoni pizzas, there will be 2 cheese pizzas.

'Ella's friend Alex suggests they order a total of 15 pizzas. If Ella takes Alex's advice, how many of each type of pizza would she need to buy in to order to keep the 3:2 ratio?'[32]

A good first step for your learner is to read the problem using the *Picture-At-Punctuation* technique described in Chapter 13. Have your learner describe the mental images they created while reading the problem; if they are distorted, incomplete, or contain superfluous information, gently guide your learner as appropriate. Once your learner has a set of mental imagery that fully and accurately depicts the problem, they could create 3 pepperoni pizzas and 2 cheese pizzas out of plasticine. Guide your learner to make the two types of pizza visually different from each other.

---

[32] Generated at https://chat.openai.com/

Now, you could have your learner lay out all the pizzas in a row.

Ask, 'How many?' and elicit the answer, 'Five.' Ask how many of the five are pepperoni (3) and how many cheese (2).

Next, ask your learner how many pizzas Alex suggested to Ella that she buy; elicit the answer, 'Fifteen'.

Say to your learner, 'You can make more than these five pizzas, but each time, you need to make another complete row that is a copy of this one [point to the row of pizzas already made]. Can you see how many rows you would need altogether to have fifteen pizzas?' If your learner has been through a Davis Maths Mastery Programme and is familiar with the Davis multiplication grid, they should quickly recognise that three rows will do the trick.

Once this has been recognised, invite your learner to make the additional rows. As needed, remind your learner that each row needs to be a copy of the existing row, with the same number of pepperoni pizzas and cheese pizzas as were in the first row. (Most learners will recognise very quickly what needs to be done, in which case no reminders will be needed.)

With your learner, revisit the last paragraph of the problem above:

'Ella's friend Alex suggests they order a total of 15 pizzas. If Ella takes Alex's advice, how many of each type of pizza would she need to buy in to order to keep the 3:2 ratio?'

Most likely, your learner will simply 'see' the answer without requiring further prompting. If they don't, guide them to count the total number of pizzas (15), then count the number of pepperoni pizzas (9) and the number of cheese pizzas (6).

As appropriate, allow your learner to write the answer.

Your learner could then move on to further problems, such as the one here:

'Mia is planning to make a fruit punch for her friends. She needs to mix orange juice and pineapple juice in a ratio of 2:3. If she wants to make a total of 5 cups of fruit punch, how much orange juice and how much pineapple juice should she use?'

If Picture-At-Punctuation and mental imagery are sufficient for your learner to confidently predict the answer, allow that to happen. At any sign of difficulty or confusion, return to the clay and allow your learner to make a model along the principles outlined above.

If needed, you can gradually explore with your learner ratio problems of increasing complexity, returning to the clay at any signs of confusion that cannot be resolved through 'picturing'.

## Quadratic Expressions — Expanding the Brackets

Quadratic expressions are another area of mathematics that can confound a picture-thinker if they are explained purely in words. One of the early skills taught in this domain is how to remove the brackets from a *factorised* expression such as this one:

$(x + 1)(x + 2)$

This expression is called 'factorised' because each of the expressions inside the brackets is a factor of the total value. Factors are amounts that are multiplied together to create a new resulting amount. In the above expression, one-more-than-$x$ is to be multiplied by two-more-than-$x$.

Again, that might work for a word thinker. But for a picture thinker, we need to do better than that.

Consider why these expressions are called 'quadratic' in the first place. 'Quadratic' means 'square'. Mathematically, a square number is the result of multiplying a number by itself. In geometry and in the real world, a square is a right-angled shape with four sides of equal length. Once we expand the factorised expression in a picture thinking way, we are going to 'see', not just a square, but also a rectangle.

Start by checking if your learner is familiar with the principle that $x$ represents an unknown amount. If your learner seems uncertain, do the procedure for simple algebra scripted earlier in this chapter, or devise a process of your own for making this clear.

Then check if your learner is aware that the area of a rectangle is calculated as its length multiplied by its width. If your learner seems hesitant or uncertain about this principle, explore it on some squared paper or graph paper. For example, if using paper with 1cm$^2$ squares, you could draw (or have your learner draw) a rectangle that encompasses 3 x 2 such squares:

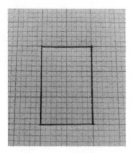

Then you could say to your learner: 'Imagine these are little tiles that you need to cover a room in a doll's house. The room is 3cm long [point along one of the lengths] and 2cm wide [point along one of the widths]. How many of these tiles [point to the squares] will you need?'

If your learner expresses hesitation, invite them to count the squares. Your learner should confidently conclude that they will need 6 tiles.

Say to your learner, 'The size of a two-dimensional surface, such as a floor, wall or ceiling, is called its *area*. Such surfaces can come in different shapes. When the shape is a rectangle, its area is always its length multiplied by its width. So here: 3 [*point along the length*] times 2 [*point along the width*] equals 6 [*point at the 6 squares*]. Does that make sense?'

Note: as appropriate, you might also discuss the unit of measurement $cm^2$. This is not necessary for understanding quadratic expressions but could be useful knowledge for geometry.

Another note: if your learner has completed a Davis Maths Mastery Programme, you might point out or discuss the visual similarity between the area calculation in squares and the ball multiplication grid used in Davis Maths Mastery Exercise 6 (see Chapter 11 above).

Finally, check if your learner knows that a square number is the result when a number is multiplied by itself. If necessary, return to the graph paper and draw various squares, e.g. a 2cm x 2cm square consisting of four 1cm² squares; a 3 x 3 square; a 4 x 4 square, and so on.

Once your learner has a clear concept of the above two principles, have your learner make a short strip of clay that is 1cm wide. If necessary, use a ruler or tape measure to measure the width.

Ask your learner to refrain from measuring the strip's length. Say to your learner, 'You have made an unmeasured length. Because it is unmeasured, we can say it is unknown. In algebra, we can use $x$ to represent an unknown amount. So let's agree that this strip is $x$cm long.'

Now, would you agree that the surface of this strip is a long, thin rectangle? To calculate the area of a rectangle, you multiply the length by the width. This strip is x cm long. We also know it is 1cm wide, because you measured that, right? So the area of the strip is $x$ times 1.'

Elicit from your learner that $x$ times 1 equals $x$; if not immediately obvious, discuss. Have your learner etch $x$ onto the top of the strip.

Then say to your learner, 'Now, make some more strips like this one: they should all be the same length and the same width. Make 4 more strips, so that with this one, there will be 5 altogether.'

Once this is done, have your learner etch $x$ onto the top of each remaining strip. Then have your learner move all the strips except one out of the working area on the table.

Say to your learner, 'Now make a square slab out of plasticine. The slab should be $x$cm long and $x$cm wide. Use this strip [point to the $x$-strip that was not put to one side] to measure the width and the length of the slab.'

Once the slab is made, say to your learner, 'Now you need to state the area of the slab. It is a square that is $x$cm long and $x$cm wide. We still don't know how long $x$cm is, but we do know that the area of the square will be $x$ times $x$. This can be written as $x^2$. Does that make sense?'

Clarify as needed. Once this idea makes sense, have your learner etch $x^2$ onto the slab.

Say to your learner, 'Now you are going to try to make a rectangle out of all these pieces.' Guide your learner to place the $x^2$ slab bottom left, three $x$'s directly above, then two $x$'s directly to the right of the slab. There will be a 2cm x 3cm gap in the top right hand corner.

Say to your learner, 'These pieces can't make a complete rectangle, so we need some more pieces to fill in the gap. Start by making a square slab that is 1cm long and 1cm wide.'

Have your learner make such a piece.

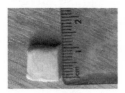

Discuss how the area of the piece is 1cm x 1cm which is 1cm$^2$. Have your learner etch a *1* onto the top of the piece.

Have your learner place the new '1' piece in the corner of the gap in the rectangular structure.

Ask, 'Can you see how many of these pieces you will need to complete the rectangle?'

If your learner confidently says 'Six,' say, 'Ok – go ahead and make more pieces until you have 6, and use them to complete the rectangle.' If your learner is uncertain how many pieces will be required, have them make further '1' pieces one at a time and add them to the structure until the rectangle is complete. Have your learner etch a '1' onto each of the new pieces.

Now point along the bottom edge of the construction, from the bottom left to the bottom right corner, and ask, 'How long?' If your learner doesn't immediately understand, you could ask, 'If a small creature like an ant was walking from here [point to the bottom left corner] to here [point to the bottom right corner], how far would it travel?' Give gentle guidance as needed until your learner realises that the distance is $x + 2$. Have your learner make '$x + 2$' out of clay rope and then place it along the bottom of the rectangle.

Now point up the left edge, from the bottom left to the top left corner, and ask, 'How long?' Your learner will most likely recognise that the answer is $x + 3$; give gentle guidance as needed. Have your learner make '$x + 3$' out of clay rope and then place it along the left edge of the rectangle.

Say, 'Ok, now let's look at the area of the rectangle. The area of a rectangle is its length times its width, right? Here, the length is $x + 3$ and the width is $x + 2$, right. So the area will be this [*point at the length*] times this [*point at the*

*width*]. When we want to write this on paper, because the length and the width cannot be expressed as a single number, we need to put them each in brackets.'

Guide your learner to write $(x + 3)(x + 2)$ on paper. Have your learner write an equal sign after the two sets of brackets.

Say to your learner, 'However, there is another way of writing the area, without using brackets. You just need to count the pieces. How many $x^2$ slabs do you have?' Elicit the answer: '1'. 'Now, how many $x$-strips do you have?' As needed, guide your learner to count the total number of strips both above and to the right of the $x^2$ slab, to reach the answer, '5 $x$-strips'. 'Now, how many *1*'s do you have?' Elicit the answer, '6'.

Say to your learner, 'After the equals sign, write down what you just told me.' As needed, guide your learner to recognise that they need to write: $x^2 + 5x + 6$.

$$(x + 3)(x + 2) = x^2 + 5x + 6$$

Your learner now has a mental image of what a quadratic expression means, depicted as a two-dimensional shape. Now, your learner may be taught various strategies for expanding the brackets of these expressions. A common one is the acronym *FOIL* for the various multiplications that need to be done (*front-*

*outside-inside-last*). Another option, used by my colleague Angie Beer, is to move the area/rectangle method from clay onto paper, as shown here:

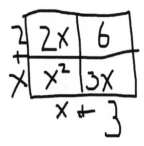

Whereas, in the past, such strategies would have been confusing because they were existing in a 'meaning vacuum', now your learner has an experiential frame of reference that will make the standard classroom procedures more accessible.

I have seen this principle work again and again with picture-thinking learners. Imagine asking a child to write a story about the seaside when they have never seen the sea. Now imagine taking that child on a field trip to the seaside, then asking them to write a story about the seaside. When you get out the plasticine to explore principles such as those covered in this chapter, you are essentially taking your learner to the mathematical seaside.

# Chapter 15: Building a Mathematical Recovery Plan

It is arguable whether it is worse to have dyslexic difficulties with literacy or dyscalculic difficulties with numeracy. Because reading and writing are ubiquitous in classroom-based learning, any unusual difficulties with these skills will be obvious and, potentially, shameful. Not being able to read or write is acutely embarrassing and can be very damaging to self-esteem. At the same time, because literacy difficulties are difficult to hide, there is much more awareness of dyslexia in society and among teachers than there is of dyscalculia. While understanding of dyslexia remains limited and some of the strategies applied to it misguided, a dyslexic individual in a developed economy has a reasonable chance of being detected, diagnosed, supported with adjustments to the learning, testing and/or working environment, and protected legally against discrimination.

Dyscalculics may sometimes experience less pain than dyslexics, because their difficulties are less stigmatised. Speaking into dictation software to check the spelling of a birthday card greeting for a colleague might raise an eyebrow; whipping out a calculator to check your share of the lunch bill will probably not. Difficulties with reading and writing will affect your maths and science exams; difficulties with numeracy will rarely make a difference in English, History or Religious Studies.

Yet precisely because of this, being dyscalculic today is like being vegan in the 1980s: hardly anybody knows what it means, let alone where it comes from. Levels of both diagnosis and support are at far lower levels than for dyslexia, and the somewhat pedantic distinctions made between dyscalculia and '*mathsisjusthardia*' probably do not help in an already barren diagnostic environment. It is more than likely that a dyscalculic individual will go through life not knowing that they have a diagnosable difficulty with maths and numbers. That puts the dyscalculic experience in the same ball court where dyslexia was 40 years ago. And as we know, individuals with undetected learning difficulties tend to conclude, oh so wrongly, that they are 'just stupid'.

Just as the diagnosis of number difficulties lags way behind that of dyslexia, so an understanding of what dyscalculia is and how to help has a long way to go. Just as with dyslexia, an effective intervention strategy needs to be based on respect for, and curiosity about, the natural thinking and learning strengths of the individual. Dyscalculics are not 'broken' or mathematical 'no-hopers'; rather, they think and learn differently from those who are doing just fine in the maths classroom.

Understanding why some learners have not naturally acquired concepts such as *cause, effect, time, sequence* and/or *order* from their environment is the first step.

Finding creative, explorative media that help a learner to discover these concepts for themselves is the starting point in assisting the development of mathematical thinking. Davis Concept Mastery, as described earlier in this book and in 'The Gift of Learning' by Ronald Davis, is a great way of doing this.

After this is done, a learner needs to experience the principle behind each mathematical operation creatively, resulting in the ability to picture the underlying meaning and purpose. Once this has occurred, a learner can usually start to solve examples of the given operation on paper, with confidence and with an average to above-average rate of accuracy. Previously, it was not the mental apparatus to do mathematics that was missing, but rather the right set of experiences for an individual who thinks differently from their classmates.

The advent of new learning technologies should provide some great new opportunities to make mathematical operations more visual — provided that those designing the platforms are equipped with a working understanding of how dyscalculic thinking differs from that of the numerically neurotypical. Whether learning is taking place in a digital or a physical environment, educators should keep in view the key principle that unlocks learning for the neurodiverse: if a person is to resolve persistent confusion in their learning, they will only do so by re-creating the learning material for themselves. Plasticine clay trumps flashcards every time. In the words of Ronald Davis:

*'The creative process and the learning process, if not the same thing, are so closely associated, we will never be able to separate them.'*

It is time to set struggling mathematicians free from the assumption that they will never be friends with numbers. It is time to tailor mathematical learning to the way the learner thinks.

'When someone masters something, it becomes a part of that person. It becomes part of the individual's thought and creative process. It adds the quality of its essence to all subsequent thought and creativity of the individual.'

- Ronald Davis, author, *The Gift of Dyslexia, The Gift of Learning.*

# Bibliography

Alloway, T. & Alloway, R., 2010. Investigating the predictive roles of working memory and IQ in academic attainment.. *Journal of Experimental Child Psychology,* 106(1), pp. 20-29.

Baddeley, A., 1986. *Working Memory.* Oxford: Clarendon Press / Oxford University Press.

British Dyslexia Association, 2023. *Dyscalculia.* [Online] Available at: https://www.bdadyslexia.org.uk/dyscalculia [Accessed 31 August 2023].

Davis, R. D. & Braun, E. M., 2003. *The Gift of Learning: Proven New Methods for Correcting ADD, Math & Handwriting Problems.* August 2003 ed. New York: Perigee / Penguin Putnam.

Davis, R. D. & Braun, E. M., 2010. *The Gift of Dyslexia: Why Some of the Brighest People Can't Read and How They Can Learn.* 3rd Revised Edition ed. London: Souvenir Press.

Department for Business, Innovation and Skills, 2012. *The 2011 Skills for Life Survey: a Survey of Literacy, Numeracy, and ICT Levels in England,* London: Department for Business, Innovation and Skills (UK).

Einstein, A., 1995. *Ideas And Opinions*. 3rd edition ed. New York: Crown Publishing Group.

Engelbrecht, R. J., 2005. *The effect of the Ron Davis programme on the reading ability and psychological functioning of children*. [Online]
Available at: http://bin.ddai.us/dys/docs/Engelbrecht-2005-Masters-Thesis.pdf
[Accessed 31 August 2023].

Fanari, R., Meloni, C. & Massidda, D., 2019. Visual and Spatial Working Memory Abilities Predict Early Math Skills: A Longitudinal Study. *Frontiers in Psychology*, Volume 10.

Gardner, H., 2011. *Frames of Mind: The Theory of Multiple Intelligences*. 3rd edition ed. New York: Basic Books.

Gross-Tsur, V., Manor, O. & Shalev, R., 1996. Developmental dyscalculia: prevalence and demographic features. *Developmental Medicine and Child Neurology*, 38(1), pp. 25-33.

Guzmán, B., Rodríguez, C., Sepúlveda, F. & Ferreira, R. A., 2019. Number Sense Abilities, Working Memory and RAN: A Longitudinal Approximation of Typical and Atypical Development in Chilean Children. *Revista de Psicodidáctica*, 24(1), pp. 62-70.

Halmos, P., 1968. Mathematics as a Creative Art. *American Scientist*, 56(4), pp. 375-389.

International Dyslexia Learning Solutions Limited, 2021. *6 superpowers of Dyscalculia*. [Online]
Available at: https://idlsgroup.com/news/superpowers-

of-dyscalculia/
[Accessed 31 August 2023].

Klein, J. S. & Bisanz, J., 2000. Preschoolers Doing Arithmetic: The Concepts Are Willing but the Working Memory Is Weak. *Canadian Journal of Experimental Psychology,* 54(2), pp. 105-116.

Kyttälä, M., 2008. Visuospatial working memory in adolescents with poor performance in mathematics: variation depending on reading skills. *Educational Psychology,* 20(3), pp. 65-76.

Kyttälä, M. et al., 2003. Visuospatial working memory and early numeracy. *Educational and Child Psychology,* 20(3), pp. 65-76.

Mikaye, A. & Shah, P., 1999. *Models of working memory: Mechanisms of active maintenance and executive control..* Cambridge: Cambridge University Press.

National Numeracy, 2019. *Numerate Nation? What the UK thinks about numbers,* Brighton: National Numeracy.

Norton, E. & Wolf, M., 2012. Rapid Automatized Naming (RAN) and Reading Fluency: Implications for Understanding and Treatment of Reading Disabilities. *Annual Review of Psychology,* pp. 427-452.

Nunes, T., Bryant, P., Barros, R. & Sylva, K., 2012. The relative importance of two different mathematical abilities to mathematical achievement. *British Journal of Educational Psychology,* 82(1), pp. 136-156.

Psychology Today, 2021. *Dyscalculia.* [Online]
Available at:
https://www.psychologytoday.com/gb/conditions/dysca
lculia
[Accessed 31 August 2023].

Singh, M., 2021. *7 Famous People With Dyscalculia.*
[Online]
Available at: https://numberdyslexia.com/7-famous-people-with-dyscalculia/
[Accessed 31 August 2023].

SpLD Assessments Standards Committee (SASC), 2019.
*SASC Guidance on assessment of Dyscalculia and Maths Difficulties within other Specific Learning Difficulties.*
[Online]
Available at:
https://sasc.org.uk/media/215bhkbr/dyscalculia-maths-difficulties-assessment-sasc-nov-2019.pdf
[Accessed 30 August 2023].

Whitehead, R. N., 2017. *Why Tyrannosaurus But Not If? The Dyslexic Blueprint for the Future of Education.* 1st edition ed. Malvern: Create-A-Word Books.

Willburger, E. et al., 2008. Naming speed in dyslexia and dyscalculia.. *Learning and Individual Differences,* Volume 18, p. 224–236.

Witt, M., 2006. Do Different Mathematical Operations Involve Different Components Of The Working Memory Model?. *Proceedings of the British Society for Research into Learning Mathematics,* 26(3), pp. 65-70.

# INDEX

# Going Further

# Also by Richard Whitehead

There are some bright and creative people who thrive in conventional learning environments. There are others — just as bright and creative — who do not. For too long, our educational systems have been unable to comprehend how dyslexics think and, therefore, how they learn. What is more, by failing to engage with the innovative traits of the dyslexic mind, our schools are missing priceless opportunities to enrich the learning of all.

'**Why** *Tyrannosaurus* **But Not** *If?*' takes as its starting point a curious phenomenon: the mistakes made by many dyslexic readers on small, common words. Drawing on a wide range of knowledge and research, and with especial regard to the work of Ronald Davis, this is a book of know-how about dyslexia that empower teachers, parents and dyslexics alike. Compelling insights into the workings of the dyslexic mind are coupled with proven practical strategies, exemplified through scripted examples of teaching modules.

**www.whyty.co.uk**

# More Davis Methods books

**The Gift of Dyslexia: Why Some of the Brightest People Can't Read and How They Can Learn**

**Ronald Davis**
Davis' seminal work on the nature of dyslexic thinking talent. Unique insights into dyslexia from an author who is himself dyslexic. Includes a complete how-to guide for all the basic Davis techniques.

**The Gift Of Learning: Proven New Methods for Correcting ADD, Math & Handwriting Problems**

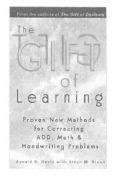

**Ronald Davis**
Davis' second book builds on the principles outlined in The Gift of Dyslexia to outline strategies for addressing ADHD and Maths Difficulties. Also includes strategies for resolving handwriting difficulties that have been resistant to conventional tuition (dysgraphia).

**Autism and the Seeds of Change**

**Abigail Marshall, Ronald Davis**
An in-depth look at a revolutionary approach to empower individuals with autism, and provide the understanding and tools needed to achieve their full potential. The Davis Autism Approach is uniquely geared to the autistic perspective and enables each person to make sense of their world and the motivations and behaviours of others around them.

All and more available at **www.dyslexia-books.co.uk**

# Getting Help through the Davis® Methods

Davis Dyslexia Correction Facilitators help people who struggle with:

- Reading
- Spelling
- Writing
- Maths

- Time-Keeping
- Attention focus
- Organisation
- Coordination

**Davis Autism Approach/Concepts for Life Facilitators** help neurodiverse individuals with autistic and/or executive function challenges.

**To Search For A Davis Provider Near You, Go To:**

## https://www.davismethod.org/

# Help For Parents

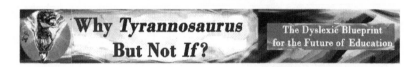

**Why *Tyrannosaurus* But Not *If*?**

The Dyslexic Blueprint for the Future of Education

## Dyslexia-inspired strategies
## For parents of all struggling learners

**Six practical support sessions that make parents the best helpers they can be**

## What you will learn

### Session 1: Confused?
Your journey as the parent of a bright but struggling learner.

The role of confusion in a learning difficulty.

The Davis 'Release' Procedure.

### Session 2: Gifts and Problems
The talents that go with learning difficulties.

How can a talent cause a problem?

Word thinking and picture thinking.

### Session 3: How do dyslexics think and learn?
The concept of 'disorientation' and its role in a learning difficulty.

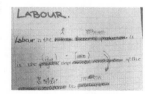

The problem with if.
The Davis 'Create-A-Word'
procedure.

## Session 4: Learning for Picture Thinkers
Visualisation for reading comprehension
Punctuation as a reading skill
Retention of what has been read
Why Clay?
The Davis 'Picture-At-Punctuation' and 'Symbol Mastery'
techniques.

## Session 5: Going Deeper
'Picture-At-Punctuation': fiction
and fact.
Dictionaries: their power for picture-thinkers.
'Symbol Mastery' on subject-specific vocabulary.
Picturing technical definitions.

## Session 6: Pulling it all together
Comprehensive course review.
Creating a complete support strategy for
your bright but struggling child

For details of courses near you, go to
## https://www.whyty.co.uk/

# The *Gift of Dyslexia* Workshop

The **Gift of Dyslexia Workshop** is a four-day introduction to the basic theories, principles and application of all the procedures described in Ronald Davis's internationally best-selling book, The Gift of Dyslexia, and more. Training is done with a combination of lectures, demonstrations, group practice, and question and answer sessions.

**Participants will learn:**

- How the Davis procedures were developed.

- How to screen for the 'gift of dyslexia' and establish a symptoms profile.

- How to help dyslexics eliminate perceptual disorientation and focus their attention.

- Special techniques for working with people who do not visualize well or have ADHD symptoms.

- How to incorporate and use proven methods for reducing confusion and mistakes in a classroom, home-schooling, tutoring or therapeutic setting.

- How to structure a Davis Dyslexia Programme.

## Who Should Attend?

- ✓ Parents
- ✓ Home educators
- ✓ Teachers
- ✓ SENDCOS
- ✓ LEARNING Support Staff
- ✓ Tutors
- ✓ Psychologists
- ✓ CounselLors
- ✓ Speech therapists
- ✓ Occupational Therapists
- ✓ Trainers
- ✓ Researchers
- ✓ Career Guidance Counsellors
- ✓ Anyone interested in helping others correct their dyslexia

For details of workshops near you, go to
**https://www.davistraining.info/**

**'I don't understand it: He can read *'tyrannosaurus'*, but he gets stuck on *'if'*!!'**

**Would you like to:**

- Grasp the reasons why some bright children may struggle to acquire basic academic skills;
- Use these insights to make an incisive difference to the abilities, well-being and prospects of these children in your classroom;
- Acquire insights and approaches that enable you to stimulate both academically able and academically challenged children at the same time;
- Give disruptive and impulsive children better control of their focus and behavior;
- Make a valuable difference to children who, while they may be academically able, have difficulty in areas such as sitting still, controlling hand-eye coordination, succeeding at sports, learning from consequences, or reading people?

**Sign up to my *free* online course for teachers and parents and struggling learners. Ask your child's teachers to sign up too.**

**www.whytyrannosaurusbutnotif.com**

# Richard Whitehead

Richard originally discovered the Davis methods when looking for a solution for the son of some friends. He is a Davis Workshop Presenter and Training Specialist and has delivered lectures and teaching workshops on the Davis methods in countries as diverse as Iceland, Estonia, Ireland, Italy, Portugal, Poland, the United States, India, South Africa, New Zealand and Israel.

Richard's extensive background in education has included time spent teaching in both the adult and mainstream secondary educational sectors. From 2009 – 2019, Richard occupied various positions at Malvern College, a flourishing independent secondary boarding school in Worcestershire, UK which specialises in the International Baccalaureate for its international students. Richard was Head of German for three years, IB Theory of Knowledge Coordinator for five years, a Deputy Housemaster for two years, Special Educational Needs Coordinator for six years and Peer Mentoring Scheme Coordinator for eight years. He is an accredited Specialist SpLD Teacher Assessor.

Richard has written articles on the dyslexic learning style for publications as diverse as Literacy Today, Green Parent Magazine and Personnel Today magazine and he has recorded video presentations on dyslexia for the Dystalk project (http://www.dystalk.com). He has conducted webinars on multi-sensory learning for Operation Diversity, the University of Chester and the SEND Group. In March 2022 and March 2023, Richard was a guest speaker at the Dyslexia Show in Birmingham.

Made in the USA
Monee, IL
28 December 2023

50729242R00132